EU Law and Human Rights

LAMMY BETTEN
Professor of European Law
University of Exeter

and

NICHOLAS GRIEF
Professor of the Law of International Organisations
Bournemouth University

LONGMAN
LONDON AND NEW YORK

Addison Wesley Longman Limited
Edinburgh Gate
Harlow, Essex CM20 2JE
England

and Associated Companies throughout the world

*Published in the United States of America
by Addison Wesley Longman Inc., New York*

© Addison Wesley Longman Limited 1998

The right of Lammy Betten and Nicholas Grief to be identified as authors of this
Work has been asserted by them in accordance with the Copyright, Designs and
Patents Act 1988.

First published 1998

ISBN 0 582 287162 Paper

British Library Cataloguing-in-Publication Data

A catalogue record for this book is
available from the British Library

Library of Congress Cataloging-in-Publication Data

Betten, Lammy.
EU law and human rights / Lammy Betten and Nicholas Grief.
p.   cm. -- (European law series)
Includes bibliographical references and index.
ISBN 0-582-28716-2 (pbk.)
1. Civil rights--European Union countries. 2. Human rights.
I. Grief, Nicholas. II. Title. III. Series.
KJE5132.B45 1998
341.4'81--dc21   98-11058
                                                             CIP

Set by 7 in 10/12 Sabon
Produced through Longman Malaysia, CLP

Contents

General Editor's Preface

The Longman European Law Series is the first comprehensive series of topic-based books on EC Law aimed primarily at a student readership, though I have no doubt that they will also be found useful by academic colleagues and interested practitioners. It has become more and more difficult for a single course or a single book to deal comprehensively with all the major topics of Community law, and the intention of this series is to enable students and teachers to 'mix and match' topics which they find to be of interest; it may also be hoped that the publication of this series will encourage the study of areas of Community law which have historically been neglected in degree courses. However, while the series may have a student readership in mind, the authors have been encouraged to take an academic and critical approach, placing each topic in its overall Community context, and also in its socio-economic and political context where relevant.

In examining the protection of human rights in the European Union, this book necessarily considers the relationship between EC Law and the European Convention on Human rights (a matter of particular interest given the pending incorporation of the Convention into the legal systems of the UK). It also explains the protection of fundamental rights in the context of the development of general principles of Community Law, and the evolution of specific provisions in the Treaty on European Union, and in Agreements between the EC and third countries. It gives me particular pleasure that this book has been written by one of my former colleagues at Exeter and my successor at Exeter.

J.A. Usher.

Abbreviations

AC	Appeal Cases
ACP	African, Caribbean and Pacific countries
All ER	All England Law Reports
All ER (EC)	All England Law Reports (European Cases)
ASEAN	Association of South East Asian Nations
CFI	Court of First Instance
CFSP	Common Foreign and Security Policy
CJHA	Cooperation in the Fields of Justice and Home Affairs
CMLR	Common Market Law Reports
CMLRev	Common Market Law Review
CSCE	Conference on Security and Cooperation in Europe
DR	Decisions and Reports (European Commission of Human Rights)
EAEC	European Atomic Energy Community
EC	European Community
EC Bull	Bulletin of the European Communities
ECHR	European Convention on Human Rights
ECJ	European Court of Justice
ECOSOC	UN Economic and Social Council (or, depending on the context, Economic and Social Committee of the European Communities)
ECR	European Court Reports
ECSC	European Coal and Steel Community
EEA	European Economic Area
EEC	European Economic Community
EHRLR	European Human Rights Law Review
EHRR	European Human Rights Reports
ESC	European Social Charter

ETUC	European Confederation of Trade Unions
EU	European Union
FAO	Food and Agricultural Organisation
HL	House of Lords
HLSC	House of Lords Select Committee (on the European Communities)
HRLJ	Human Rights Law Journal
ICCPR	International Covenant on Civil and Political Rights
ICESCR	International Covenant on Economic, Social and Cultural Rights
ICJ	International Court of Justice
IGC	Intergovernmental Conference
ILO	International Labour Organisation
IRLR	Industrial Relations Law Reports
LIEI	Legal Issues of European Integration
NGO	Non-Governmental Organisation
NQHR	Netherlands Quarterly of Human Rights
OAS	Organisation of American States
OAU	Organisation of African Unity
OECD	Organisation for Economic Cooperation and Development
OEEC	Organisation for European Economic Cooperation
OJ	Official Journal (of the European Communities)
QB	Queen's Bench Reports
SEA	Single European Act
TEC	Treaty establishing the European Community
TEU	Treaty on European Union
TLR	Times Law Reports
UN	United Nations
UNESCO	UN Educational, Scientific and Cultural Organisation
UNICE	Union of Confederations of Industry and Employersof Europe
UNICEF	UN Children's Fund
WHO	World Health Organisation
WLR	Weekly Law Reports
YECHR	Yearbook of the European Convention on Human Rights
YEL	Yearbook of European Law

Table of Cases

TABLE OF CASES

xi

Introduction

This book is about the protection of human rights in the European Union. Until 1st November 1993, when the Treaty on European Union (TEU, better known as the Maastricht Treaty) came into force, developments in human rights protection necessarily occurred only in the context of the three European Communities, *viz* the European Coal and Steel Community (ECSC), the European Economic Community (EEC)[1] and the European Atomic Energy Community (EAEC). Those developments have continued since the entry into force of the Maastricht Treaty, which amended the three foundation Treaties and established new forms of co-operation between the High Contracting Parties (the Member States). The Maastricht Treaty included provisions on human rights in the European Union, provisions which have since been strengthened by the 1997 Amsterdam Treaty.[2]

It should be emphasised at the outset that the legal orders of the European Communities, on the one hand, and the European Union, on the other, must be distinguished. Apart from a number of common[3] and final[4] provisions, the Maastricht Treaty comprises three pillars: the first consisting of the three foundation Treaties as amended, the second on a Common Foreign and Security Policy (CFSP)[5] and the third on Co-operation in the fields of Justice and Home Affairs (CJHA).[6] The difference between the

---

1 Renamed the European Community (EC) by the Maastricht Treaty.
2 The Amsterdam Treaty was signed on 2 October 1997. Where appropriate, we refer to the consolidated versions of the TEU and TEC.
3 Arts A–F.
4 Arts L–S.
5 Art J (Title V).
6 Art K (Title VI).

first pillar and the two new pillars is that only the former is supranational; the others are intergovernmental. That is to say, the term 'Community law' applies only to the three foundation Treaties as amended and to acts adopted in pursuance of those Treaties. The principles of Community law, such as supremacy and direct effect, do not apply to the pillars which are based on intergovernmental co-operation.

This fundamental difference between the component parts of the European Union affects the system of human rights protection. Whereas within the framework of Community law human rights constrain both the Community itself and the Member States, the general human rights provisions in the intergovernmental elements of the Maastricht Treaty do not have this effect. For all practical purposes the ECJ currently has no jurisdiction over activities which fall within the spheres of CFSP and CJHA.[7] It also lacks jurisdiction over Art F(2) TEU, which commits the Union to respecting fundamental rights as guaranteed by the European Convention on Human Rights (ECHR) and as they result from the constitutional traditions common to the Member States, as general principles of Community law. The Court itself has drawn attention to the fact that legal problems may arise because of the denial of judicial protection to individuals affected by the Union's activities, especially in the context of CJHA. At present, any complaint of an infringement of the Convention in that sphere would have to be lodged in Strasbourg against the Member State or States concerned. Under the Amsterdam Treaty, however, a large part of the original third pillar of the TEU will become subject to Community rules and ECJ jurisdiction. In addition, there will be limited judicial control of activities under Title VI, jurisdiction over Art F(2) with regard to action of the institutions and a procedure for enforcing the principles upon which the Union is founded, which include respect for human rights.

Although this book concerns the protection of human rights in the European Union, it should be noted that respect for human rights is a key element of the Community's relations with third countries.[8] The first reference to human rights in the body of a contractual document was in Art 5 of the fourth Lomé (ACP–EEC)

---

[7] See Art L TEU.
[8] See further D McGoldrick, *International Relations Law of the European Union* (Longman, 1997).

2

Convention, 1989.[9] In May 1995, in response to a Commission communication, the Council approved a suspension mechanism to be included in agreements with third countries to enable the Community to react immediately in the event of serious and persistent human rights violations.[10] As the Economic and Social Committee has observed, however, such agreements do not yet include adequate arrangements for monitoring compliance with human rights clauses.[11]

The working method used in this book is essentially one of increasing specificity. In order to put the subject-matter in context, we begin by outlining the system and significance of the international protection of human rights. Accordingly, the first two chapters explain the general system of protection at global (Chapter 1) and European (Chapter 2) level. In Chapter 3, the development of human rights protection within the European Communities is examined, with particular reference to the European Court of Justice (ECJ). Chapter 4 analyses the domestic impact of those developments in the Member States; we focus on the legal implications for the United Kingdom.

Next, we turn to the relationship between EU law and the European Convention on Human Rights. First, we consider the significance of the Convention and of Strasbourg case law for the interpretation and application of EU law, thereby illustrating the Convention's importance to EU lawyers (Chapter 5). Then we examine the question of the accession of the European Communities to the ECHR and the European Social Charter (Chapter 6). Finally, we discuss the implications for the protection of human rights in the EU of the new Amsterdam Treaty[12] and the proposed incorporation of the European Convention into UK law (Chapter 7).

---

9 Art 5(1) of the Convention stated, *inter alia*, that 'development policy and cooperation are closely linked with the respect for and enjoyment of fundamental human rights'.

10 See Bull EC 5-1995, 1.2.2 and 1.2.3.

11 Economic and Social Committee of the European Communities, Opinion on 'The European Union and the external dimension of human rights policy', 23–24 April 1997 (CES 474/97).

12 The Treaty is subject to ratification by the High Contracting Parties in accordance with their respective constitutional requirements. It will enter into force on the first day of the second month following that in which the instrument of ratification is deposited by the last signatory State to fulfil that formality.

CHAPTER ONE

The international protection of human rights

1. The origin of the concept of human rights

While some scholars argue that the Old Testament gives early examples of the concept of human rights, the historical basis of the development of such concept is usually set in Greek antiquity. On the basis of Natural Law, Greek philosophers began to accept the idea of unchangeable laws in society. One of their central theses was that all human beings are equal. The idea of equality was also accepted by the School of Stoa, which influenced the development of Roman law concepts. The development of the concept of human rights continued in the Middle Ages, though with the focus on (privileged) classes of people rather than on individuals. According to some authors, the ideas of freedom and equality, which lie at the heart of the concept of human rights, owe their origin to the emergence of ownership of property.[1]

This raises the point that conceptual thinking about human rights cannot be considered in isolation from the society in which it developed. To the modern student of human rights, it may seem strange to point to the ideas of equality in Greek and Roman societies of which slavery was an accepted feature. Although it is not possible in this book to explore the theoretical depths of these ideologies, some awareness of their development is appropriate, since it helps to clarify the use of certain terminology.

At the end of the eighteenth century, human rights thinking focused very much on the so-called 'classic' human rights, i.e. the inalienable rights of the individual. They were conceived as freedoms

---

[1] See e.g. Imre Szabo, 'Historical Foundations of Human Rights and Subsequent Developments', in Karel Vasak (ed.) *The International Dimensions of Human Rights* (Greenwood Press, 1982), vol 1, p 13.

rather than rights. Their basic characteristic was non-interference by the State: they created an area of freedom for the individual with which public authorities could not interfere. The first codifications of human rights – the English Bill of Rights (1689), the American Declaration of Independence (1776) and the French *Déclaration des droits de l'homme et du citoyen* (1789) – were based on these ideas. One of the most important legal theorists on the inalienable rights which influenced the substance of these instruments was the British philosopher, John Locke.

Another category of human rights was developed in the twentieth century on the basis of the ideas of socialist philosophers such as Saint Simon and Karl Marx. They held that 'classic' human rights were of little use to the majority of people, who lived in appalling circumstances. With others, they developed a category of so-called economic and social rights or 'modern' human rights. In contrast with the first category, these rights demanded government intervention, which, by creating policies aimed at ensuring economic and social rights, would achieve more equitable societies. The first codifications of this category of rights can be found in the 1917 Mexican Constitution and the 1918 Constitution of the former Soviet Union, followed by the 1919 Constitution of Weimar. The constitutions of most Member States of the European Union contain express recognition of both classic (civil and political) and modern (economic and social) rights. In the United Kingdom, however, the constitutional protection of human rights through an enforceable Bill of Rights is only now being established.[2]

In the 1960s, after a period of decolonialisation, the so-called 'third world countries' argued for another category of rights to be protected, i.e. those of 'peoples', also called 'the right to development', 'community rights' or 'solidarity rights'.[3] The rights in this category reflect the impoverished position in which these countries find themselves in terms of economic power, in sharp contrast to those countries which, by exploiting third world resources, have steadily increased their riches.

The growth of the number of small States (mainly due to decolonisation) represented in the United Nations, the egalitarian voting system in the UN General Assembly and sympathy for the third

---

2   See Chapters 2 and 7.
3   For a critical analysis, see Philip Alston, 'A Third Generation of Solidarity Rights: Progressive Development or Obfuscation of International Human Rights Law?' (1982) 29 Netherlands International Law Review 307.

world countries' quest in some quarters of the western world resulted in the adoption of the 1986 Declaration on Development. This was seen as an important document in the framework of the establishment of a New International Economic Order.[4] The Declaration includes provisions on the sovereignty of natural resources, the redistribution of economic wealth in general and the economic rights and duties of States. This third category of human rights is included in the 1981 African Charter on Human and Peoples' Rights. Although no specific examples can be found in universal human rights documents, the International Covenants, part of the Universal Bill of Rights, both contain a reference to the rights of peoples.[5]

In spite of the different historical and ideological backgrounds of these various categories of rights, they all form part of the modern concept of human rights. For progressive improvement of the protection of human dignity, respect for all these different kinds of human rights is necessary. Their effect in law may be different[6] but they are all equally important.

1.1 Terminology

Above we referred to the sometimes confusing terminology with which students of human rights have to cope: human rights, fundamental rights, basic rights, basic human rights, civic rights,[7] constitutional rights, rights of man, rights of citizens, etc. Each of these different terms has its particular meaning. However, there is disagreement over the exact meaning of the different terms. For instance, all agree that there are rights which individuals can exercise on their own; they are, not surprisingly, called individual rights. Rights which, of necessity, have to be exercised with others are called collective rights. Disagreement starts when it comes to putting rights into a particular category. Some put civil and political rights in the 'individual' category and economic and social rights in the 'collective' category. However, the distinction is not always straightforward. It could be argued that the right to marry, a civil right, is as collective as the right to strike, a social right.

The terms 'human rights' and 'fundamental rights' suggest

---

4   UN General Assembly, Resolution 41/128, 4 December 1986.
5   See below.
6   See below.
7   See Chapter 7.

different concepts. The term 'fundamental rights' indicates the basic character of the rights. It represents the concept of the *Grundnorm*, the basic norm in the light of which every other norm must be reviewed. This term is more common in German law and literature. To illustrate this confusion of terms, however, note that the section on fundamental rights (*Grundrechte*) in the German constitution opens with a reference to human rights (*Menschenrechte*). The term 'human rights' reflects more the idea that these are the inalienable rights of human beings, with which no State can interfere.

For the title of this book we have used the term 'human rights', which is easier to understand in common law systems where the term 'fundamental rights' has no conceptual significance. However, such a choice may be criticised as the European Court of Justice generally refers to 'fundamental rights'. This can be explained by the important influence of German courts on the development of the ECJ's human rights case law. Accordingly, when we quote from the Court's case law, we often use the term 'fundamental rights'. Keep in mind, therefore, that both terms are used in the book.

Other terminology which may be confusing is that used to describe States which are parties to international human rights treaties. All treaties have their own terminology: e.g. States Parties, High Contracting Parties. These terms refer to States which have signed and ratified (or acceded to) the treaty in question; thereby becoming bound by it. In this book we shall use the terminology which is used in the particular treaty to which we are referring. If we are not referring to any treaty in particular, we use the term 'contracting parties'.

Contracting parties must be distinguished from Member States. That term refers to States which are members of an intergovernmental organisation, like the Council of Europe or the United Nations. Membership of such organisations does not necessarily mean that the States in question are parties to the treaties of those organisations. It is possible to be a member of the Council of Europe, for instance, without having ratified the European Convention on Human Rights or the European Social Charter. Becoming a member of an international organisation and the ratification of a treaty adopted within the framework of that organisation are two separate legal acts. Needless to say, the legal effect of membership of the European Communities is completely different from that of other organisations. The EC legal order lies somewhere between domestic legal orders and international law.

2. The international protection of human rights

2.1 Introduction

The protection of human rights in international treaties represented a new phenomenon in international law, which had traditionally focused only on relations and obligations between States. International treaties formulated obligations for the contracting parties as to the treatment of each other's subjects but did not create rights for individuals. States were obliged to ensure minimum standards of protection within their jurisdiction. Such treaties on diplomatic protection were for a long time the only attention which individuals received in international law.

The first international treaties on the protection of human rights date from the early nineteenth century when a number of bilateral and multilateral treaties on the abolition of slavery were concluded in Europe. The earliest treaties concluded within the framework of international organisations date from the end of the First World War, when various declarations were adopted within the League of Nations (the predecessor of the United Nations), e.g. on the protection of minorities in eastern Europe.

More important, perhaps, are the economic and social rights mentioned in the 1919 Constitution of the International Labour Organisation (ILO) which forms part of the Peace Treaty of Versailles.[8] The ILO Constitution proclaims that social justice is a precondition for lasting peace. It was the first international treaty to recognise the freedoms of association and expression as well as the right to equal treatment. However, it was after the Second World War that comprehensive work on the international protection of human rights began in earnest. The atrocities committed during the 1939–45 war, which caused the deaths of millions of people and traumatised other millions for the rest of their lives, strongly motivated post-war efforts to adopt international standards for the protection of human rights.

---

8 Chapter XIII.

One of the most crucial aspects of international human rights protection is the method of implementation of those provisions. It is one thing for States to agree on international standards; it is quite another for them to agree that they will be legally bound by those standards or, going one step further, allow individuals and/ or other States to invoke those standards before national and/or international courts. It is in this respect, particularly, that human rights treaties heralded a new era in international law. Never before had individuals played such an important role in the implementation of the international obligations of sovereign States. This role depends very much on the status and effect of international human rights provisions in national legal orders.

2.2 Legal status of international human rights standards

The status and effect of international human rights standards depend on a number of issues. They include the nature of the right in question, the effect of the treaty or standard in national law and recognition of the jurisdiction of international courts.

2.2.1 The legal character of the standards

Assuming that a treaty is duly ratified and creates legal obligations for the contracting parties, the first thing to look at is the way in which the standard is formulated. There are essentially two stereotypical ways of formulating human rights: as an obligation for a contracting party or as a right for the individual. The former involves the creation of legally-binding obligations for the contracting parties, but individuals cannot rely on the treaty's provisions before a national (or international) court. The contracting parties' obligations consist of creating certain conditions or pursuing certain policies or programmes to realise the enjoyment of these rights, which is why they are sometimes called 'programmatic rights' or 'progressive rights'. The important thing is that individuals cannot invoke those rights before their national courts. Their governments' policies may be criticised by international supervisory bodies. Their governments may even be accused of failing to fulfil their obligations under the relevant treaty. However, these standards do not create any corresponding rights for the individual.

The second category creates so-called 'legal' or 'justiciable' rights. These are formulated in such a way that they can be invoked in court by individuals.[9] If included in international treaties, they gain, provided that other conditions are fulfilled,[10] 'self-executing' effect. One of the main conditions of self-executing treaty provisions is that they be clear and unconditional and require no further government action. The term 'self-executing' can be compared with 'direct effect' in the context of Community law.

Traditionally, whereas civil and political rights were seen as justiciable, i.e. rights which could be invoked by the individual against the public authorities, economic and social rights were generally regarded as 'programmatic'. As we saw above, the distinction lay in the fact that the former demanded non-interference by public authorities whereas the latter required active intervention.

For example, the right to freedom of expression is a justiciable right: it creates an area of freedom for the individual with which public authorities cannot interfere. Therefore, if an individual expresses an opinion contrary to official policy, there can be no punishment. (Of course, this freedom is not absolute; it does not give the individual the right unjustly to accuse other persons of, for instance, illegal behaviour.) If an individual is sent to prison for having expressed an opinion, he or she should be able to claim a violation of the right to freedom of expression. The judge can then decide whether or not there has been a violation. On the other hand, the right to work is an example of a programmatic right in that it creates an obligation for the contracting parties *inter alia* to pursue an employment policy which offers maximum employment opportunities. A State can be reprimanded for not following such a policy, but individuals cannot go to court to claim that the government has violated their right to work, nor can the right be invoked in the event of unfair dismissal by an employer.

This difference in character demands different methods of enforcement, which means that different methods of supervision of the enforcement of international human rights treaties are needed. In general, civil and political rights treaties, which contain self-executing rights, usually have a system of judicial enforcement in national courts[11] as well as before an international body such as

---

[9] A distinction should be drawn between 'adversarial justiciability' and 'inquisitorial justiciability'. See further Michael K Addo, 'Justiciability Reexamined' in *Economic, Social and Cultural Rights: Progress and Achievement* (Beddard and Hill eds) (Macmillan, 1992), p 93.

[10] See section 2.2.2 below.

[11] See, however, section 2.2.2 below.

the UN Human Rights Committee or the European Court of Human Rights.

Treaties containing 'programmatic' rights do not usually contain individual complaints procedures. The supervision of their implementation is limited to a system of reporting, in the framework of which States periodically report to international bodies on their implementation of the relevant treaty. It should be emphasised that such treaties do impose legally binding obligations on States; it is just that individuals have no direct recourse to the corresponding rights. In other words, the fact that an international standard is not self-executing does not mean that States are not legally obliged to implement the standard in their domestic legal orders.

Some systems involve an amalgamation of complaints and reporting procedures. See, for instance, the supervisory procedures in the framework of the ILO, which consist of a number of interrelated complaints and reporting procedures.

It was the need for different supervisory mechanisms which led to the adoption, at universal as well as regional levels, of separate treaties for different categories of rights. On the one hand, the civil and political rights which were regarded as 'justiciable' non-interference rights; on the other, the economic, social and cultural rights which were regarded as 'programmatic' or 'progressive' rights.

However, the neat distinction once drawn between 'justiciable' civil and political rights and 'non-justiciable' economic and social rights is no longer generally accepted in legal writing.[12] Nowadays, it is customary to look at the definition of a provision rather than at its label. For example, the right to strike, labelled as a social right, is now accepted as justiciable. It does not require government action; on the contrary, for its full realisation it requires non-interference by public authorities. That makes the right to strike a justiciable right which can be invoked in court against a public authority.

For all categories of rights it is true that their exercise can be restricted in order to safeguard other fundamental values. However, the possibilities of limiting the exercise of human rights are themselves restricted. Any limitation must be based on and justified by the relevant treaty itself. See, for instance, the second paragraphs of Arts 8-11 of the European Convention on Human Rights

[12] See Addo, op cit.

(ECHR) and Art 31 of the European Social Charter (ESC). In general, restrictions on the exercise of human rights must be prescribed by law and necessary in a democratic society to safeguard such values as the rights and freedoms of others, public order and public safety, health or morals.

States can derogate from their obligations under human rights treaties in time of war or other public emergency.[13] There are, however, some rights which are required to be respected at all times. They include the right of individuals to be free from torture or inhuman or degrading treatment or punishment and the right not to be held in slavery or servitude, as well as the principle of legality expressed in the maxim *nulla poena sine lege* (no one should be convicted or punished except for breach of existing law).

2.2.2 The relationship between international and national law

Even if civil and political rights are generally formulated in a 'self-executing' fashion, ratification of the instruments containing such rights does not automatically create justiciable rights for the citizens of all contracting parties. This is because the effect of those provisions in the national legal orders depends on the relevant constitutional provisions.

There are, broadly speaking, two different views on the relationship between national and international law: the monist view and the dualist view. The monist theory regards both areas of law as part of the same system. Upon ratification, the treaty in question automatically becomes part of the national system and the self-executing provisions of the treaty can be invoked in national courts. In monist countries, most of the 'classic' (civil and political) human rights provisions are self-executing.

Most States have adopted the monist view. In practice, this means that, upon ratification, an international treaty becomes effective in national law without any further act. Germany, Austria and Italy have adopted a qualified form of monism in that, upon ratification, the treaty gains the status of a national act.

The dualist theory sees national law and international law as separate areas. Therefore, for an international treaty to become effective in the domestic legal order, a national statute to that effect must be adopted. That national act is not related to ratification; it

---

13 See e.g. Art 15 ECHR.

is a separate enactment of the treaty. If such an act is not adopted, the treaty does not become part of domestic law and the individual cannot invoke its provisions in the national courts. The United Kingdom (as well as Commonwealth and Scandinavian countries) follows the dualist view. So far, no international human rights treaties have gained the status of domestic law in the United Kingdom. Accordingly, their provisions cannot be invoked in British courts. However, this situation will change when the British government fulfils its plans to incorporate the ECHR into UK law.[14]

2.2.3 International jurisdiction/ locus standi

The justiciability of international human rights provisions in national law must be distinguished from the right of individuals to bring complaints before an an international court or committee. This 'right of complaint' or 'right of petition' depends on whether or not the State in question has accepted the jurisdiction of such international body. It is an option, not an obligation, for States to accept the individual's right of petition: see Art 25 of the European Convention[15] and the First Optional Protocol to the International Covenant on Civil and Political Rights.[16] Under Protocol No 11 to the European Convention, however, acceptance of the right of petition will cease to be optional. The conditions to be fulfilled before a complaint can be declared admissible are rather strict.[17]

In conclusion, therefore, the effect of international human rights provisions on the legal position of the individual depends not only on whether or not the provision is a self-executing one enshrining 'justiciable' rights, but also on whether the constitutional system of the particular State recognises the status of international human rights in national law.

3. The United Nations system

The basis for all post-Second World War human rights treaties is the Charter of the United Nations Organisation, which was estab-

14 See Chapter 7.
15 See Chapter 2, section 3.2.
16 See section 3.3.2 below.
17 See Chapter 2, section 3.2.

lished in 1945 as the successor of the League of Nations (1919–1946).

3.1 UN Charter

The UN Charter itself does not specify in detail the individual human rights which are to be protected by civilised nations. However, it does more than simply state the principle of human rights in its preamble. In Art 1(3) it calls for international co-operation 'in promoting and encouraging respect for human rights and for fundamental freedoms for all without distinction as to race, sex, language or religion'. In Art 55 it repeats this commitment to the promotion of universal respect for human rights.

The Charter also confers several functions on UN bodies with a view to achieving these aims. Under Art 13(1), for example, the General Assembly's functions include initiating studies and making recommendations for the purpose of 'assisting in the realisation of human rights and fundamental freedoms for all without distinction'. Similarly, Art 55 provides that with a view to the creation of the conditions necessary for peaceful and friendly international relations, the UN shall promote *inter alia* 'universal respect for, and observance of, human rights and fundamental freedoms for all without distinction'. By Art 56, all Member States undertake to cooperate with the UN for the achievement of the purposes set forth in Art 55. Article 60 stipulates that responsibility for the discharge of the UN's functions under Arts 55 and 56 shall be vested in the General Assembly and the Economic and Social Council (ECOSOC). One of the functions of ECOSOC is to set up commissions in economic and social fields and for the promotion of human rights.[18]

Whether or not the Charter imposes an obligation upon UN Member States to respect human rights,[19] specific instruments have been adopted to create a system of human rights protection. In particular, the Universal Declaration of Human Rights, the International Covenant on Civil and Political Rights (ICCPR), and the

---

[18] Art 68.
[19] Cf. *Advisory Opinion on the Legal Consequences for States of the Continued Presence of South Africa in Namibia (South West Africa) Notwithstanding Security Council Resolution 276 (1970)* ICJ Reports 1971, p 16, at p 57, para 131.

International Covenant on Economic, Social and Cultural Rights (ICESCR).[20]

3.2 The Universal Declaration of Human Rights, 1948

The Universal Declaration of Human Rights lists no fewer than 29 human rights from both the 'classic' and the 'modern' categories, aimed an ensuring universal respect for and observance of human rights and fundamental freedoms. According to its preamble, the Declaration is to be seen as 'a common standard of achievement for all peoples and nations, to the end that every individual and every organ of society . . . shall strive . . . to promote respect for these rights and freedoms'.

The juxtaposition of civil and political and economic, social and cultural rights was possible only because the Declaration was not drafted as a legally binding instrument, so the question of supervising its implementation did not arise. In spite of (or perhaps because of) its declaratory character, it has been a very important source of inspiration for the drafting of other human rights instruments at universal and regional as well as national levels. While not legally binding as such, the Declaration is an authoritative guide to the interpretation of the UN Charter. Moreover, since it has been accepted by virtually all States, some scholars argue that it has become binding as a source of international law.[21] It is said to represent 'international custom, as evidence of a general practice accepted as law'.[22]

In 1968, at an international conference to mark the twentieth anniversary of the Universal Declaration, the Proclamation of Tehran was adopted. Endorsed by the UN General Assembly,[23] this proclaims the urgency of addressing situations of political injustice, such as apartheid, colonialism and the gap between rich and poor. It also refers to gross violations of human rights and declares illiteracy and discrimination against women to be major obstacles to the full realisation of human rights. By reaffirming the importance of the Universal Declaration, the Proclamation endorses the legally binding character of the Declaration's principles. At

---

20 See Michael O'Flaherty, *Human Rights and the UN: Practice Before the Treaty Bodies* (Sweet & Maxwell, 1996).
21 See e.g. L B Sohn, 'The Universal Declaration of Human Rights' (1968) Journal of the International Commission of Jurists, Special Issue, pp 25–6.
22 Art 38(1)(b) of the Statute of the International Court of Justice.
23 Resolution 2442 (XXIII), 19 December 1968.

the same time, it indicates that the legal recognition of human rights is not sufficient to confront injustice in the world.

The Proclamation of Tehran also emphasises the third category of human rights, i.e. the rights of peoples. Not surprisingly, the importance of such rights is asserted by third-world countries in particular. These nations exerted strong pressure in the 1960s, when the decolonisation process was nearing completion. The first thing they did was to sign up for UN membership, to become fully recognised as members of the universal 'family of States'. In view of the egalitarian voting system in the General Assembly, this gives the vote of States like Togo and Tobago – with fewer than 100,000 inhabitants and a minimal contribution to the UN budget of less than 0.5 per cent – a weighting equal to that of the United States, which pays a quarter of the total UN budget.

3.3 The International Covenants, 1966

Whereas the Universal Declaration was adopted as a non-binding instrument, it was generally recognised that there was a need to formulate a human rights instrument which would be legally binding. The above-mentioned dispute about the difference between civil and political rights, on the one hand, and economic and social rights, on the other, resulted in the creation of two international treaties: the International Covenant on Civil and Political Rights (ICCPR, the 'Political Covenant') and the International Covenant on Economic, Social and Cultural Rights (ICESCR, the 'Social Covenant').

The two Covenants were adopted by the UN General Assembly on 16 December 1966.[24] Both were to enter into force once 35 countries had ratified.[25] This was achieved on 23 March 1976 for the Political Covenant and on 3 January 1976 for the Social Covenant.

3.3.1 International Covenant on Civil and Political Rights

The Political Covenant consists of a preamble and six Parts and is supplemented by two Optional Protocols.[26] Interestingly, the text

---

[24] General Assembly, Resolution 2200 (XXI).
[25] Art 49(1) ICCPR, Art 27(1) ICESCR.
[26] The First Optional Protocol is considered below. A Second Optional Protocol on the abolition of the death penalty was concluded in 1989 and entered into force in 1991.

of the preambles of both Covenants is similar; both recognise the equal importance of economic, social and cultural as well as civil and political rights. This represents a compromise between those countries which wanted both categories of rights to be included in one instrument and those which wanted two separate instruments.

Part I of the Political Covenant contains another political compromise since it enshrines the above-mentioned third generation right of peoples, *inter alia*, to self-determination. Part II sets out the obligations which States Parties undertake upon ratification. Part III contains the substantive rights. Arts 6–27 enumerate a wide range of human rights and fundamental freedoms many of which are, in one form or another, focused on the right to life, liberty and security of person. Other rights are concerned with the guarantee of a fair and public trial, the freedom of thought and expression, freedom of association, etc. Part IV establishes a Human Rights Committee, consisting of independent experts, nominated and elected by the States Parties.[27] The Committee's task is to examine the States Parties' reports on the implementation of the Covenant.[28] The UN's specialised agencies[29] are consulted on reports relating to their specific tasks.

Art 41 of the Covenant enables a State Party to lodge complaints about another State Party. However, both States must accept the Human Rights Committee's competence to receive and consider such complaints. This system of inter-State complaints must be distinguished from the right of individuals to lodge complaints against States Parties, which is regulated by the First Optional Protocol.

Parts V and VI contain procedural rules which are customary in international treaties of this kind. Slightly out of place here, perhaps, is Art 47, which stipulates that '[n]othing in the present Covenant shall be interpreted as impairing the right of all peoples to enjoy and utilise fully and freely their natural wealth and resources'. This was inserted at the request of third-world nations.

---

27 Arts 28–45 ICCPR. See Dominic McGoldrick, *The Human Rights Committee: Its Role in the Development of the International Covenant on Civil and Political Rights* (Oxford, 1994).
28 Art 40 ICCPR.
29 See section 3.4 below.

3.3.2 The First Optional Protocol to the ICCPR

The First Optional Protocol gives States Parties to the Political Covenant the option to accept the right of individuals to lodge complaints about violations of their human rights under that Covenant. Complaints can only be brought against States Parties which have recognised the competence of the Human Rights Committee to receive and examine such complaints. Arts 1–6 of the Protocol set out the conditions and the procedure to be followed.

Nearly 90 States have ratified or otherwise acceded to the First Optional Protocol. They include all Member States of the EU except the United Kingdom, which declined to ratify on the grounds that in some respects the Protocol compares unfavourably with the procedure for lodging individual complaints under Art 25 ECHR.[30] Since the Protocol's entry into force, the Human Rights Committee has received several hundred complaints.[31] However, in only a handful of cases has a violation of the Covenant been found. Most complaints have been declared inadmissible or have failed to establish a violation.

3.3.3 International Covenant on Economic, Social and Cultural Rights

The Social Covenant consists of a preamble[32] and five Parts. The text of Parts I and II is similar to that of the Political Covenant. Part III contains ten provisions[33] on economic, social and cultural rights. Their formulation differs markedly from that of the provisions in the Political Covenant. This gives a clue to the different ways in which the implementation of the respective provisions is to be realised. Whereas many provisions of the Political Covenant stipulate that '[e]veryone shall have the right to',[34] thereby creating justiciable rights, the provisions of the Social Covenant create obligations for States Parties which cannot be invoked by individuals. The general formula in this Covenant is '[t]he States Parties recognise the right of everyone to', for instance, the enjoyment of just and favourable conditions of work.[35] The argument is that such

---

30 N J Grief 'The International Protection of Human Rights: Standard-setting and Enforcement by the United Nations and the Council of Europe' (1983) 16 Bracton Law Journal 41, 51.
31 See O'Flaherty, *op cit*, p 48.
32 See above.
33 Arts 6–15.
34 See e.g. Art 18 ICCPR.
35 Art 7 ICESCR.

conditions have to be created by way of public policy. Accordingly, the only obligation arising from this Covenant is the obligation upon the State to formulate and implement such policies. Although this argument remains valid for a number of these rights, some of them have moved into (or have always been in) the category of justiciable rights; e.g. the right to form and join a trade union, which also forms part of the Political Covenant.[36]

Apart from the obvious difference in the contents of the norms, the most significant difference between the two Covenants lies in their systems of supervision. This is not a reference to the effect of the instruments in domestic legal orders, but to the methods of ensuring that the Contracting Parties fulfil their obligations which, under both Covenants, are binding in international law.

The reporting system under the Social Covenant has been completely reorganised due to its initial malfunctioning. Under Art 16(1), States Parties must submit regular reports to the UN Secretary-General, who transmits them to the Economic and Social Council (ECOSOC). The Covenant then sets out an elaborate system of consultation (here, too, specialised agencies are consulted), recommendations and general reports. In short, ECOSOC was entrusted with the task of considering the national reports which were to be submitted in accordance with a rather haphazard system.[37] A Sessional Working Group was set up to assist ECOSOC in the consideration of the reports. At first it consisted of representatives of States Parties. In 1982 it became the Sessional Working Group of Governmental Experts, consisting of experts selected from a list put forward by the Covenant's States Parties.

The whole system collapsed in 1984, when the first surveys were published. They had been severely criticised for being 'cursory, superficial and politicised'.[38] In 1985, ECOSOC created the Committee on Economic, Social and Cultural Rights to assist it in monitoring the implementation of the Covenant. The Committee consists of independent experts from all over the world, representing different social and legal systems.[39] While it has operated more successfully than its predecessors, it has still not overcome the rather negative attitude of a considerable number of States Par-

---

36 Art 8 ICESR and Art 22 ICCPR.
37 General Assembly, Resolution 1988 (LX) of 11 May 1976.
38 Commentary by the International Commission of Jurists, ICJ Review, No 27 (1981). p 26.
39 See Flaherty, op cit, p 53.

ties which either send incomplete reports and inadequate representatives for the oral hearings, or fail to report at all. In order to reach conclusions in spite of the lack of support by States Parties, the Committee has adopted the practice of giving 'general comments' which are intended to develop a fuller appreciation of the obligations under the Covenant.[40]

Despite the Committee's attempts to overcome the problem of supervising implementation of the Covenant, the procedure continues to suffer from unpopularity, not only because of States' reluctance to fulfil their obligations but also because of a lack of publicity. If people are aware of the existence and significance of the Social Covenant, very few have any knowledge of the Committee's work. This is a lot shared, as we shall see, by European bodies involved in monitoring respect for economic and social rights.

3.4 Specific treaties and specialised agencies

Apart from the general human rights instruments adopted under the auspices of the United Nations, a number of important specific treaties and conventions have been adopted within the framework of the Organisation or its specialised agencies.

The UN has adopted treaties on the protection of specific groups, such as the 1926, 1949 and 1956 Treaties prohibiting slavery, traffic in persons and exploitation of prostitution; the 1973 International Convention on the Suppression and Punishment of the Crime of Apartheid, the 1979 Convention on the Elimination of All Forms of Discrimination Against Women, the 1989 Convention on the Rights of the Child and the 1991 International Convention on the Protection of All Migrant Workers and Members of Their Families.

Although these treaties have been widely ratified, this does not necessarily mean that they are effective in achieving their goals. One of their main defects is the ineffective supervision of implementation. None of the above treaties allows individuals to lodge complaints against States which violate their rights. Most of them have reporting procedures, but these seldom enjoy the respect which they were presumably intended to have. Nevertheless, such treaties do influence law-making at national level and are

40 ECOSOC Resolution 1990/45, para 10.

used as points of reference in the context of the general human rights treaties.

Under the UN system, a number of organisations with specific aims were established or brought into the UN 'family'. These are the so-called specialised agencies. Well-known examples are the United Nations Children's Fund (UNICEF), the United Nations Economic, Social and Cultural Organisation (UNESCO), the Food and Agricultural Organisation (FAO), the World Health Organisation (WHO) and the International Labour Organisation (ILO). The latter will be discussed in some detail here, because it has created a catalogue of international human rights standards concerning the protection of workers.

3.4.1 The International Labour Organisation (ILO)

As its name indicates, the ILO's work is focused on labour. Since its inception in 1919, the ILO has adopted about 180 conventions and recommendations. They are all aimed at the protection of the livelihood of the major part of the world's population, i.e. access to employment, employment conditions and protection after employment. A number of the conventions establish basic human rights: the 1947 and 1948 Freedom of Association, Right to Organise and Right to Free Collective Bargaining Conventions;[41] the 1930 and 1957 Abolition of Forced Labour Conventions;[42] and the 1958 Equality in Employment and Occupation Convention.[43]

These conventions are widely ratified. Each year, heated discussions on alleged violations of their principles take place in the Conference Committee which examines the application of the conventions and recommendations.[44] One of the outstanding features of the ILO is the tripartite composition of nearly all the institutions of the Organisation. This means that governments, employers' organisations and trade unions are involved in the drafting as well as the supervision of the implementation of the standards. The ILO supervisory system combines reporting and complaint systems, in-

---

[41] Conventions Nos 87 and 98, followed by Conventions Nos 151 (1978) and 154 (1981).
[42] Conventions Nos 29 and 105, to be followed by a special Child Labour Convention, which will probably be adopted in 1999.
[43] Convention No 111.
[44] These discussions, which take place at the annual session of the International Labour Conference, are reported in the Records of Proceedings of the Conference, published by the International Labour Office in Geneva.

volving independent experts, politicians, employers and trade union representatives.

The ILO system, which has worked quite well throughout this century, has recently been criticised by employers. They have attacked both the methods of standard-setting and the supervisory system. As to the latter, they allege that the independent experts have too much influence. As to the former, they want to put an end to the regularity with which the ILO adopts new norms as a matter of course each year. This practice has now come under revision, along with the large number of overlapping conventions. At its 1997 session, the International Labour Conference adopted an amendment to the ILO Constitution which makes it possible for obsolete conventions to be abrogated.

Although often excluded from general treatises on human rights protection, the ILO has one of the most sophisticated and effective implementation systems at the level of global international organisations.

4. Regional protection of human rights

4.1 Introduction

While national representatives were meeting in New York with a view to rebuilding world society, at regional level various initiatives were taken, not only to promote human rights but also to establish institutional cooperation in the economic field. The region which went fastest and furthest was Europe, which had been hit hardest by the effects of the Second World War, both in terms of human loss and economic devastation.

4.2 Europe

Whereas the idea of European integration is by no means a modern one, it certainly became, in the eyes of many, an inevitability. Many people saw European integration as the only way of preventing a recurrence of those disastrous armed conflicts between European States.

During the Second World War, the combined European resistance movements issued a statement in which they pleaded for a Federal Union between the European peoples (1944). The British

Prime Minister, Sir Winston Churchill, had coined the term 'United States of Europe' in his famous Zurich speech in 1942. The Netherlands, Belgium and Luxembourg actually concluded an economic union between them before the war was over (1944).

After the war, the priority was to create conditions to safeguard the common European heritage of democracy, freedom and dignity of the individual, as well as to facilitate economic and social progress.[45] Work started on two levels: one was mainly concerned with rebuilding the economy by way of close cooperation between European States; the other was to establish the importance of the protection of human rights and fundamental freedoms, which had been violated in an unprecedented (but unfortunately not unrepeatable) way during the war.

Post-war activities aimed at economic recovery and cooperation took place within the framework of the Marshall Plan, the Organisation of European Economic Cooperation (OEEC)[46] and, of course, the European Communities. While it may be submitted that the establishment of the European Communities implicitly sought to avoid future violations of human rights by creating better economic conditions, the protection of human rights as a specific concern of Community law was considered but ultimately rejected. The drafters of the Community Treaties decided, first, that this was an issue to be dealt with in the context of the Council of Europe; and, secondly, that human rights would not be violated by activities within the context of the EC Treaties. We now know that this was a serious misjudgement which caused many problems in the European Community, the functioning of which has been threatened precisely because of this issue.[47]

Post-war efforts aimed at the protection of human rights and fundamental freedoms occurred within the Council of Europe. While there is an abundance of literature about the European Communities, there is very little on the Council of Europe. This indicates, once again, that economic issues have a higher priority than human rights protection.

The Council of Europe was established in 1950, with its seat in Strasbourg. Its institutional structure consists of a Parliamentary Assembly, a Committee of Ministers and a Secretary-General. The

---

45 See Art 1 of the Statute of the Council of Europe.
46 Reconstituted in 1960 as the Organisation of Economic Co-operation and Development (OECD).
47 See Chapter 3.

work of these bodies is not widely known. The Council of Europe's main achievement is its most important instrument, the European Convention for the Protection of Human Rights and Fundamental Freedoms (1950), better known as the European Convention on Human Rights (ECHR) or simply the European Convention.[48]

The Council's social treaty, the European Social Charter (1961), tends to suffer the same fate as the Council itself. Very few people are familiar with the Charter. Most (including leading politicians) confuse it with the European Community Charter of Fundamental Social Rights for Workers.

This lamentable position may be redeemed slightly now that membership of the Council of Europe has become a reality for States in eastern Europe. A large number of middle and eastern European States[49] have recently joined the Council of Europe, bringing its membership up to 40. However, whereas most of these countries have ratified the European Convention, so far only Poland and Romania have ratified the European Social Charter.[50]

All EU Member States are also members of the Council of Europe. For the moment, however, the Council enjoys much more popularity in countries of eastern Europe than in those of western Europe. The former see membership of the Council of Europe as a first step towards membership of the European Union.

4.3 Other regions

Because of their limited relevance for the subject-matter of this book, we shall only mention briefly the human rights instruments adopted within the framework of other regional organisations.

4.3.1 America

The Organisation of American States (OAS), established in 1948 in Bogotá, is concerned with the peace and security of the American continent (including North and South America).[51] Its basic do-

---

48 See Chapter 2.
49 Poland* (1991); Bulgaria* (1992); Estonia*, Lithuania*, Slovenia*, Czech Republic*, Slovakia*, Romania* (1993); Latvia, Albania*, Moldavia, Ukraine, Macedonia (1995); the Russian Federation and Croatia (1996). The countries with an asterisk have also ratified the ECHR.
50 By November 1997. See Chapter 2.
51 Art 4 of the Bogotá Charter.

cument is the American Declaration of the Rights and Duties of Man. It contains civil and political rights and duties, but not economic and social rights; these were added in a complementary document, the Inter-American Charter of Social Guarantees. The work of the OAS is consistently hampered by internal conflicts and little has been achieved in terms of integration.

The 1969 American Convention on Human Rights, the American version of the ECHR, has not achieved the same success as its European equivalent, even though the organisation established a Court of Human Rights in 1979. Unlike its European counterpart, however, this court cannot take binding decisions and there is no appeal from the Inter-American Commission on Human Rights which was established 20 years earlier. The Commission is the principal organ of the OAS. It can receive complaints about violations of human rights, make recommendations to Member States and report to the OAS Conference.

The Commission has examined thousands of communications on alleged human rights violations. However, at the beginning of the 1980s it was suggested that its work did not have an immediate impact on the observance of human rights in the Americas.[52] Unfortunately, this situation has not changed much. The Commission receives little media attention and the people of American countries are generally unaware of its valuable work.

4.3.2 Africa

In 1963, the Organisation of African Unity (OAU) was established in Addis Ababa. It aims at cooperation between African and Malagasy States in a number of policy areas, such as economic policy, transport, communication, health, sanitation and nutritional policy, defence and security.

At its 1981 meeting in Nairobi, the Assembly of the Heads of State and Government adopted the African Charter on Human and Peoples' Rights. The Charter comprises all of the three abovementioned categories of human rights; civil and political rights, based on the provisions of the UN instruments; economic, social and cultural rights (e.g. the right to work under equitable and

---

52 Gros Espiell, 'The Organisation of American States (OAS)', in Karel Vasak (ed), *The International Dimensions of Human Rights* (Greenwood Press, Paris, 1982), pp 548 *et seq*.

satisfactory conditions, the right to equal pay for equal work, the right to the best attainable state of physical and mental health, the right to education); and peoples's rights (e.g. the right to existence, the right to self-determination, the right to peace and security, the right to a satisfactory environment).

In 1988, a Commission was charged with the supervision of the Charter's implementation, which is based on regular reports by States Parties as well as inter-State and individual complaints of alleged violations.

4.3.3 Arab countries

The League of Arab States (1945) established a Permanent Arab Commission on Human Rights in 1969. In addition, in 1971 a draft Declaration for an Arab Charter of Human Rights was completed. Unfortunately, the draft has not yet been adopted. Consequently, the Arab Commission remains fairly insignificant in this area.

4.3.4 The Far East

There is no regional organisation or instrument focused on the protection of human rights in the Far East (Pacific Rim) region. The Association of South-East Asian nations (ASEAN), which was established in 1967, concentrates on general political and economic matters.

Legal writing in a number of Asian countries suggests that there are two reasons for the apparent lack of interest in human rights treaties and organisations in Asia. The first is that 'Asia' does not exist as a coherent regional entity. The second is that the international protection of human rights is entirely based on a western concept which is totally alien to Asian cultures.[53]

---

[53] For outspoken criticism of western attitudes to Asian countries, see Bilahari Kausikan, 'Asia's Different Standard', in Alston (ed), *Human Rights Law* (Dartmouth, 1996), pp 24 *et seq.*

CHAPTER TWO

The European Conve[...]
on Human Rights and the
European Social Charter

I. Introduction

At the 1948 Congress of Europe in The Hague, representatives of European States came together with the aim of establishing an organisation in which all of them would cooperate to construct a region where democracy and human rights would be safeguarded. As a result, the Council of Europe was established in August 1949, counting among its members most countries of Western Europe. At the first meeting of the Consultative Assembly – renamed the Parliamentary Assembly in 1973 – it was decided to start work immediately on the drafting of treaties which would serve as the basis upon which human rights protection in Europe could be guaranteed.

There was discussion as to whether all categories of human rights should be included in one instrument. Although the fundamental value of economic and social rights was recognised, it was decided to create two instruments and to begin with the guarantee of political democracy in Europe, before starting on social democracy.

Progress on civil and political rights was swift: on 4 November 1950, in Rome, the European Convention on Human Rights (ECHR or the Convention) was signed by all Council of Europe Member States. It entered into force on 3 September 1953. Work on the definition of economic and social rights progressed much more slowly. Not until 1961 was the European Social Charter (ESC or the Charter) signed in Turin. It entered into force in 1965.

At first, the number of Member States of the Council of Europe, as well as the number of ratifications of both instruments, grew very slowly. This changed dramatically after the fall of the Berlin

, which led to the dissolution of the socialist bloc. Central and stern European States immediately sought rapprochement with the West and its organisations. Many have acceded to the Council of Europe which, at the end of 1997, had 40 Member States; of these 39 have ratified the ECHR and 21 the ESC.

In this chapter, the scope and substance of both instruments will be examined. Their relationship with European Union provisions will be considered in the following chapters, where we discuss human rights protection in Community law. For now we focus on the structure, scope and effect of the Convention and the Charter.

2. The European Convention on Human Rights: structure, scope and effect in national law

2.1 Structure

The original Convention consists of a preamble, Art 1 and five Sections; it has been amended or supplemented by 11 Protocols. The preamble of the Convention reaffirms the profound belief of the Council of Europe's members—

> in those Fundamental Freedoms which are the foundation of justice and peace in the world and are best maintained on the one hand by an effective political democracy and on the other by a common understanding and observance of the Human Rights upon which they depend.

It also expresses their resolution 'to take the first steps for the collective enforcement of certain of the Rights stated in the Universal Declaration'. Art 1 requires the High Contracting Parties to secure to everyone within their jurisdiction the rights and freedoms defined in Section I of the Convention. This means that the Parties must protect everyone within their jurisdiction, irrespective of nationality or residence.[1]

Section I embodies substantive rights and freedoms: the right to life; the prohibition of torture and inhuman treatment; the prohibition of slavery and forced labour; the right to liberty and security of person; the right to a fair trial; the prohibition of retrospective penal legislation; the right to respect for privacy and family life;

---

1   See section 2.2 below.

the freedom of thought, conscience and religion; the freedom of expression; the freedom of assembly and association; and the right to marry and to found a family.[2] Added to these are the substantive rights included in certain of the Protocols to the Convention: the right to peaceful enjoyment of possessions (the right to property); the right to education; the right to free elections by secret ballot;[3] the prohibition of imprisonment for debt; the freedom of movement; the prohibition of expulsion of nationals; the prohibition of collective expulsion of aliens;[4] and abolition of the death penalty.[5]

The remaining provisions in Section I contain general principles on the enjoyment of the above-mentioned rights. Art 13 guarantees everyone whose rights and freedoms under the Convention have been violated an effective remedy before a national authority; in other words, a remedy to enforce the substance of the Convention rights and freedoms in whatever form they happen to be secured in the domestic legal order.[6] However, such a remedy is required only in respect of grievances which can be regarded as 'arguable' in terms of the Convention[7]. Art 14 provides that the enjoyment of the rights and freedoms set forth in the Convention shall be secured without discrimination on any ground. Art 15 concerns war-time and other public emergency derogations. Art 16 offers States the possibility of limiting the political activities of aliens (notwithstanding Arts 10, 11 and 14), while Arts 17 and 18 are designed to ensure that the Convention is not interpreted as allowing undue restrictions on the provisions contained in Section I.

Section II of the Convention consists of one article,[8] establishing a European Commission of Human Rights (the Commission) and a European Court of Human Rights (the Court). Section III determines the composition and functions of the Commission and Section IV does the same for the Court. Section V contains a number of final provisions.

The Convention has been amended or supplemented by 11

---

2 Arts 2–12 ECHR.
3 Protocol No 1, Arts 1–3.
4 Protocol No 4, Arts 1–4.
5 Protocol No 6, Art 1.
6 See e.g. *Aksoy* v *Turkey* (1997) 23 EHRR 553, para 95.
7 See e.g. *Halford* v *United Kingdom* (1997) 24 EHRR 523.
8 Art 19.

Protocols. Whereas some enshrine additional substantive rights, others concern procedural and institutional matters. The most important of those is Protocol No 11, which restructures the Convention's control system by providing, *inter alia*, for the merger of the Commission and the Court. An Amending Protocol, it will enter into force on 1 November 1998.[9] When the Protocol enters into force, the Convention will have a single judicial control system, instead of an amalgamation of judicial and political supervisory procedures.[10] Sections II to IV will be replaced by a new Section II and Section V will become Section III.

2.2 Scope

As mentioned above, the Convention's High Contracting Parties must respect the rights of all persons within their jurisdiction irrespective of nationality or residence. It can even be argued that the Convention applies to persons who are illegally within the jurisdiction of a State Party. It might seem strange for an individual to claim rights in a country where, legally, he or she does not exist, but that does not absolve a State from its duty to protect such a person.[11]

The Convention extends to the territories of the High Contracting Parties in so far as they have notified the Secretary-General of the Council of Europe that they accept the Convention's application to those territories for whose external relations they are responsible.[12] That provision has limited meaning nowadays, as most territories have become independent States (e.g. the former British colonies). These 'new' States can become parties to the Convention only if they are European States.[13]

2.3 Effect in national law

The effect of the Convention in domestic law depends on the relevant national constitutional provisions. If they provide that an international treaty is part of national law (the monist view), then the

---

9 In accordance with Art 4 of Protocol No 11.
10 See section 3.4 below.
11 *Cf. D v United Kingdom* (1997) 24 EHRR 423.
12 Art 63(1).
13 Art 4 of the Statute of the Council of Europe.

Convention can be invoked by individuals before their national courts. If that is not the case (the dualist view), the Convention cannot be applied directly by the national courts. As the United Kingdom represents the dualist view, British courts cannot apply the Convention as such since it has not yet been incorporated into UK law.[14]

The status and effect of the Convention in domestic law must be distinguished from the right of individuals to lodge complaints in Strasbourg. There have been many such complaints of violations of the Convention by the UK.[15] As mentioned in Chapter 1, the fact that a State has not incorporated the Convention into its domestic legal order does not prevent an individual from bringing a case before the Strasbourg institutions.

2.3.1 The effect of the Convention in the United Kingdom

At present, the Convention cannot be applied directly by British courts. However, this does not mean that it cannot be invoked by individuals. Indeed, it has to be invoked in order to fulfil the local remedies rule. One of the conditions for admissibility of a complaint in Strasbourg is that the individual must have exhausted all domestic remedies.[16] In other words, normal use must be made of domestic remedies which are likely to be adequate and effective to provide redress for the alleged wrong.[17]

Where does that leave the applicant in a British court which cannot apply the Convention's provisions directly? Art 26 is silent on this question; it simply states that all domestic remedies must be exhausted. However, Art 25 makes it clear that the individual must claim to be a victim of a violation of the rights set forth in the Convention.[18] That provision is intended to avoid the *actio popularis*. While it implies that the Convention must be invoked in national courts, it is not an obstacle to fulfilment of the local remedies rule that the Convention cannot be applied directly. In-

---

14 See further Chapter 7, section 4.
15 See S Farran, *The UK before the European Court of Human Rights* (Blackstone Press, 1996).
16 Art 26 of the original Convention; Art 35(1) of the revised Convention.
17 D J Harris, M O'Boyle and C Warbrick, *Law of the European Convention on Human Rights* (Butterworths, 1995), p 608.
18 Art 34 of the revised Convention.

deed, the fact that the Convention is not directly applicable makes a violation of the right to an effective remedy more likely. For the Convention to become effective within UK law, it would have to be incorporated by national statute. Until recently, the British government rejected the incorporation of the Convention into UK law. Incorporation was deemed unnecessary as the substance of the Convention's rights and freedoms was already considered to be respected in British law.[19] Of course, time has shown that this assessment was wide of the mark.[20] The present government is committed to incorporating the Convention into UK law.[21] However, the disadvantage of enacting a Bill of Rights through incorporation of the Convention is that the rights protected will be limited. Most other European constitutions include economic and social rights.

That apart, will incorporation make much difference to the position of the individual? It will make a difference in that the Convention will be able to be applied directly at an early stage in proceedings. This could well save the individual from having to lodge a Strasbourg petition and so from several years of uncertainty. The advantage for the European Court on Human Rights in terms of work-load as well as for the government in terms of public image should be that a smaller number of complaints will reach Strasbourg.

Incorporation should also help to create a rapport between British judges and the judges of the Strasbourg Court. Much will depend, of course, on the willingness of the former to apply the Convention's provisions fully. If we are to believe Lord Denning, a firm opponent of incorporation, that may not be easy:

> it is framed in a style which is quite contrary to anything to which we are accustomed. There are broad statements of principle and broad statements of exception – which are so broad that they are capable of giving rise to an infinity of argument . . . . They are so general that they will give rise to a multitude of cases.

He added that:

> it would be very unfortunate for our English judges . . . to be overruled by the European Court of Human Rights . . . . The

---

19 Lord Denning, *What next in the law?* (Butterworths, 1982), p 290.
20 See Farran, op cit.
21 See further Chapter 7, section 4.

English judges would have the 'feel' of the case. They will see how it should be decided in the light of the circumstances prevailing in England. They should not be overruled by judges who have no knowledge of the circumstances in England.[22]

That opinion was expressed some 15 years ago. Meanwhile, of course, British judges have gained considerable experience of interpreting and applying European law through UK membership of the European Union. Hence, they may well be less reluctant than Lord Denning suggested, despite having been 'overruled' many times by European judges; although, strictly speaking, that has concerned questions of Community law, not national law. Technically, they have not been overruled by the Strasbourg Court. That is impossible so long as the European Convention is not part of UK law and is, therefore, not applied by British judges.

2.4 Methods of interpretation

Although it respects its limitations on the basis of general principles of international law, the Strasbourg Court favours a broad interpretation of the Convention, which might not always be appreciated by the British judiciary.

An illustration of Lord Denning's fears may be found in the *Golder* case,[23] in which the Court of Human Rights interpreted the right to a fair trial[24] as including the right to access to a court. There is no express provision to that effect in the Convention. However, nor is there any provision to the contrary. The Court used the 'object and purpose' of the Convention, which is, *inter alia*, compliance with the rule of law. According to the Court, this cannot be achieved without the possibility of taking legal disputes to court. The Court thus affirmed its standing practice of interpreting the Convention in the light of its objectives. It was not surprising that the British member of the Court, Judge Fitzmaurice, strongly dissented from the Court's judgment, arguing that such a teleological interpretation was inappropriate. The Court, he said, should adhere to a more cautious interpretation of the Convention which, after all, had intruded in an area which was previously exclusively within the State's jurisdiction.

22 Op cit, at p 291.
23 *Golder* v *United Kingdom* (A/18) 1 EHRR 524.
24 Art 6 ECHR.

A second example of the 'dynamic' methods of interpretation used by the Court can be found in another British case. In *Tyrer*,[25] the Court made it clear that the Convention must be interpreted in the light of developments in society. The issue was whether corporal punishment was consistent with Art 3 of the Convention, which prohibits torture and inhuman or degrading treatment or punishment. The Court considered whether present-day society still accepted corporal punishment of school children. It was not only the intention of the drafters of the Convention which determined its objective. The general objective of the Convention should be interpreted in the light of standards currently accepted in society. Incidentally, this meets another of Lord Denning's objections to incorporation of the Convention, that it is an outdated instrument.[26]

This is not to say that the Court accepts every trend in modern society as setting the standard for the interpretation of the Convention. Although it has ruled differently than it would have done 30 years ago on homosexuals[27] and children born out of wedlock,[28] it continues to tread very carefully with regard to the rights of transsexuals.[29] Compare the case law of the European Court of Justice, which has decided that dismissal of a transsexual is a form of sex discrimination.[30]

The difficulty of the Court of Human Rights, indeed of any international court, is that standards do not develop harmoniously in all States Parties to a treaty. Accordingly, it must find a balance between the differences and the similarities. This applies to some extent to national courts, too. However, the latter can point at the legislature whose task it is to create laws consistent with current standards in society. Advocates of a more rigid interpretation of the Convention would argue that it is up to the Member States of the Council of Europe to amend the Convention so that it keeps pace with social changes.

25 *Tyrer* v *United Kingdom* (A/26) 2 EHRR 1.
26 Op cit, ibid.
27 See e.g. *Dudgeon* v *United Kingdom* (A/45) (1982) 4 EHRR 149.
28 See e.g. *Marckx* v *Belgium* (A/31) 2 EHRR 330.
29 See *Cossey* v *United Kingdom* (A/184) (1991) 13 EHRR 622, *Rees* v *United Kingdom* (A/106) (1987) 9 EHRR 56 and *X, Y and Z* v *United Kingdom* (1997) 24 EHRR 143.
30 Case C-13/94 *P* v *S and Cornwall County Council* [1996] ECR I-2143.

3. Enforcement of the European Convention

The Commission and the Court are entrusted with the task of ensuring that the High Contracting Parties observe their obligations under the Convention.[31] Although the Convention provides for a (rarely used) reporting procedure which helps to supervise its implementation,[32] there are two other procedures which are far more important and which constitute the Convention's impressive control machinery: the system of inter-State complaints and the system of individual complaints. Pending the entry into force of Protocol No 11, all complaints are considered by the Commission in the first instance and final decisions are taken either by the Court or by the Committee of Ministers of the Council of Europe.[33]

3.1 Inter-State complaints[34]

Since it is recognised that States have a general interest in the protection of human rights, the High Contracting Parties can lodge applications concerning alleged violations of the Convention by other Contracting Parties. In view of that general interest, the applicant State does not have to be a victim of the violation, nor does it have to demonstrate a particular interest in the case. The rule *'point d'intérêt, point d'action'* is interpreted broadly in this context. The interest is deemed to be the protection of human rights in general.

Inter-State complaints are rare; throughout the history of the Convention, there have been only a few dozen of this type of complaint. Quite a number have referred to the treatment of a certain category of persons by a State, e.g. the treatment of Greek Cypriots by Turkey,[35] of Greek Cypriots by the United Kingdom[36] and of Roman Catholics in Northern Ireland by the United Kingdom.[37]

---

31 Art 19 ECHR. The revised text of Art 19 refers only to the Court.
32 Art 57 of the original Convention; Art 52 of the revised Convention.
33 See further section 3.4 below.
34 Art 24 of the original Convention: Art 33 of the revised Convention.
35 *Cyprus* v *Turkey* (1997) 23 EHRR 244.
36 *Greece* v *United Kingdom*, Yearbook of the ECHR, vol 2 (1958–59), p 182.
37 *Ireland* v *United Kingdom*, Yearbook of the ECHR, vol 15 (1972), p 76. See also *Ireland* v *United Kingdom* (A/25) 2 EHRR 25.

3.2 Individual complaints[38]

By the end of 1996, the European Commission of Human Rights had received more than 12,000 complaints of alleged violations of the Convention. Over 90 per cent of those complaints had been declared inadmissible. Of the others, some were resolved by so-called friendly settlements.[39] Fewer than ten per cent of the admissible cases actually went to the Court for judgment.

There are a number of reasons why a complaint can be dismissed. This is because there are several conditions to be fulfilled before an application can be declared admissible. First of all, the complaint must be directed against a High Contracting Party which has recognised the right of individuals to lodge complaints against it. All of the Convention's High Contracting Parties currently recognise the right of individual petition. With the entry into force of Protocol No 11, there will be no choice but to do so, since recognition will cease to be optional.

Secondly, as explained above, all domestic remedies must have been exhausted. However, this rule is applied with some flexibility and without excessive formalism.[40] Of course, if restrictions inherent in the national legal system prevent a case from being taken through the full hierarchy of courts (first instance – appeal court – supreme court), local remedies are considered to have been exhausted.

Thirdly, the application must have been lodged within six months of the final domestic judgment[41] and must not be anonymous.[42] Even if the applicant has merely forgotten to sign the application, it will be dismissed. Fourthly, unless it contains relevant new information, an application must not relate to a matter which has already been examined in Strasbourg or submitted to another international supervisory body.[43]

Fifthly, the application must not be 'manifestly ill-founded'.[44] This is the most difficult of conditions. What does 'manifestly ill-founded' mean? It relates to the substance rather than the form of the petition. It does not refer to a complaint about a violation

---

38 Art 25 of the original Convention: Art 34 of the revised Convention.
39 Art 28(b) of the original Convention: Art 38(1)(b) of the revised Convention.
40 *Guzzardi v Italy* (A/39) 3 EHRR 333.
41 Art 26 of the original Convention; Art 35(1) of the revised Convention.
42 Art 27(1)(a) of the original Convention; Art 35(2)(a) of the revised Convention.
43 Art 27(1)(b) of the original Convention; Art 35(2)(b) of the revised Convention.
44 Art 27(2) of the original Convention; Art 35(3) of the revised Convention.

which falls outside the substantive scope of Convention (for instance, about the violation of a right which does not form part of the Convention). Such complaints are 'incompatible' with the Convention.[45] A manifestly ill-founded petition involves a right protected by the Convention, but the question is whether the applicant has made a *prima facie* case on the basis of such provision. For instance, an unsubstantiated complaint that a State has violated the right to freedom of expression[46] will be manifestly ill-founded because the individual has not argued any particulars of the alleged violation.

Finally, even if all of the above conditions are fulfilled, it may be decided that there is an abuse of the right of petition.[47] This happens very occasionally, usually when applicants file unfounded multiple complaints or seek to use the Convention for political propaganda purposes alleging violations which fall outside its scope.

Thus, there are quite a few hurdles to overcome before a complaint will be declared admissible, which explains the high number of cases rejected as inadmissible. Even though the first three conditions seem fairly easy to fulfil, as they are simple procedural requirements, most petitions are rejected for non-compliance with those conditions. This is less suprising than it may seem, as many complaints are sent to Strasbourg by individuals who have not consulted a lawyer. (Which is not to say that lawyers do not make mistakes in this respect.)

3.2.1 The role of the Commission

Under the original Convention, the Commission is the organ primarily charged with the establishment of facts and acts as a gateway to the Court or the Committee of Ministers. In the first place, the Commission examines all complaints for admissibility. It takes its decision by simple majority, the President having a casting vote.

Once an application is declared admissible, in the case of an individual complaint the Commission will try to reach a friendly settlement with the State(s) concerned.[48] If no friendly settlement is reached, the Commission transmits a report to the Committee of

---

[45] Art 27(2) of the original Convention; Art 35(3) of the revised Convention.
[46] Art 10 ECHR.
[47] Art 27(2) of the original Convention; Art 35(3) of the revised Convention.
[48] Art 28(b) ECHR.

Ministers in which it states its opinion as to whether the facts found disclose a breach of the Convention.[49]

Within three months of the transmission of the report to the Committee of Ministers, the case may be referred to the Court by the Commission or by the State(s) concerned: this may be the State against which the complaint has been lodged or the State of which the applicant is a national.[50] The individual(s) who submitted the application can also bring a case to the Court in accordance with Protocol No 9, which came into force in 1994.[51] With regard to an inter-State application, the applicant State can refer the case to the Court. In all cases, however, the State(s) concerned must have accepted the jurisdiction of the Court.[52] Under Protocol No 11 this will cease to be optional.

The Commission consists of as many members as there are High Contracting Parties (at present 36). There is no rule that there must be a national of each party, but in practice this has always been the case. The reason for the practice of having a Commissioner from each High Contracting Party is to ensure familiarity with the domestic legal systems represented under the Convention. Of course, such pragmatism does not exclude the involvement of third-country nationals who are familiar with one or more of the domestic legal systems.

The members of the Commission sit in their individual capacity and do not represent States.[53] They are highly qualified, independent experts elected for a period of six years and eligible for re-election[54] by the Committee of Ministers from a list drawn up by the Parliamentary Assembly on the proposal of its members. Their independence is guaranteed in a number of ways.[55] Unlike membership of the Court, until 1990 there were no formal conditions as to the qualifications of Commissioners. This was remedied by the adoption of Protocol No 8 to the Convention which sets out these conditions. The members of the Commission are usually

---

49 Art 31 ECHR.
50 Art 48 ECHR.
51 Protocol No 9 has not been accepted by France, Greece, Spain or the United Kingdom.
52 See Art 46 ECHR.
53 Art 23 ECHR.
54 Art 22(1) ECHR.
55 See e.g. Art 23 of Protocol No. 8 and Art 40 (privileges and immunities) of the Statute of the Council of Europe.

professors of law, judges or practitioners. It is only recently that the Commission has had female members.[56]

3.2.2 The role of the Court

The Court determines the merits of all cases which are referred to it, that is whether or not there has been a violation of the Convention. It will be clear from the above that, at present, a case never comes directly before the Court. It is only after the Commission has expressed its opinion that a case can be referred to the Court within three months of the Commission's report to the Committee of Ministers. Accordingly, the Court examines only a fraction of the petitions lodged in Strasbourg.

Until the entry into force of Protocol No 9 in October 1994, individuals could not refer a case to the Court. They used not to play any role in the proceedings before the Court either. When the Convention was drafted, it was feared that if individuals had *locus standi* States would not recognise the compulsory jurisdiction of the Court. Who then would put the individual's case? This question was examined in the very first case to come before the Court. In *Lawless*,[57] the Court stated that it was up to the Commission to transmit the applicant's views to the Court. The individual came a step nearer to the Court's bench in 1970, when the Court allowed the Commission to be assisted by the applicant's lawyer, who was permitted to address the Court during the hearing.[58] From then onwards, it became standing practice that the applicant's lawyers were present during the proceedings before the Court. This practice was eventually formalised in a revision of the Court's Rules of Procedure (1983). Accordingly, individuals can now participate in the proceedings on an equal footing.

The judges of the Court are elected for a period of nine years (eligible for re-election) by the Parliamentary Assembly from a list of candidates nominated by the Member States of the Council of Europe.[59] They must be of 'high moral character' and must possess the qualifications required for appointment to high judicial office in their own countries.[60] They are usually 'of age' as well. How-

---

56 At present Gro Hillestad Thune (Norwegian) and Jane Liddy (Irish).
57 *Lawless* v *Ireland (No 1)* (A/1) 1 EHRR 1.
58 *De Wilde, Ooms and Versyp* v *Belgium (No 1)* (A/12) 1 EHRR 373.
59 Art 40 ECHR.
60 Art 39(3) ECHR.

ever, Protocol No 11 requires judges to retire at the age of 70. Women judges are rare in Strasbourg. There is currently one female judge, Mrs Elisabeth Palm from Sweden.

3.3.3 The role of the Committee of Ministers

Although the Court and the Commission play the most important roles as far as the enforcement of the Convention is concerned, the Committee of Ministers must not be overlooked. While the former are judicial bodies, the Committee is political. Pending the entry into force of Protocol No 11, its principal functions under the Convention are threefold: to elect the members of the Commission,[61] to decide cases which have not been referred to the Court[62] and to supervise the execution of the Court's judgments.[63]

We saw above that cases must be referred to the Court within three months. Unless that happens, a case is currently decided by the Committee of Ministers. Which decisions are left to the Committee? In practice, those where the Commission has found no violation and the case does not raise an important Convention issue; and those where the Commission has found a violation but *either* the case raises issues which can be resolved on the basis of the Court's established case law *or* the respondent State has indicated that it accepts the Commission's opinion and is willing to take the necessary consequential measures.[64]

3.4 Protocol No 11: reform of the control machinery

The Strasbourg procedure has been under discussion for a number of years. Its main weakness is that, on average, it takes more than five years for a case to be resolved. The need to address this problem became more urgent when the number of High Contracting Parties increased, together with the number of applications, which grew from a few dozen per year in the 1960s, to a few hundred per year in the 1980s, to several thousand per year in the 1990s.

There has also been a large increase in the number of cases referred to the Court. For example, 1996 saw a 40 per cent

61 Art 21 ECHR.
62 Art 32 ECHR.
63 Art 54 ECHR.
64 Harris, O'Boyle and Warbrick, op cit, pp 692–693.

increase.[65] The Commission registered 4,758 new cases and gave decisions on 3,469 applications, only 614 of which were declared admissible. The number of Court judgments rose by 45 per cent, but at the end of the year there was still a 40 per cent increase in the number of cases pending. All in all, it became clear that neither the Commission nor the Court could cope with the workload.

The first proposals for reform aimed at creating a new two-tier system: the Commission would become a court of first instance, with the Court as a court of appeal. However, this would not have reduced delays or resolved the problem of examining a case twice. The solution considered most likely to address these problems involves creating a single, permanent court to deal with admissibility and merits. This solution was adopted in 1993 and laid down in Protocol No 11 to the Convention (1994).[66]

The new Court will deal with all individual and inter-State applications, both as regards admissibilty and merits; the former will be examined by a Chamber of three judges. Central to the new system is a Chamber of seven judges. When a case raises serious (new) questions of interpretation of the Convention, it will be transferred to a Grand Chamber of 17 judges. The Court will sit permanently and not, as is now the case, for one week per month. The procedure will be wholly judicial rather than an amalgamation of judicial and political procedures. The Committee of Ministers will cease to decide cases but will continue to supervise the execution of the Court's judgments. Finally, acceptance of the right of petition and of the Court's jurisdiction will cease to be optional.

---

65 The biggest increases in the number of applications were in Turkey (214 cases in 1995, 562 in 1996, a rise of 162 per cent); Poland (from 222 to 458, a rise of 106 per cent); Germany (223 to 334, 50 per cent); Italy (554 to 729 (32 per cent); and France (471 to 600, 27 per cent).

66 For the full text and explanatory report of the Protocol, see (1994) 17 EHRR 501. See further H G Schermers, 'The Eleventh Protocol to the European Convention on Human Rights' (1994) 19 ELRev 367.

4. The European Social Charter

4.1 Introduction

The European Social Charter was signed in 1961 in Turin by 11 Council of Europe members. It contains 19 economic and social rights, all expressed in obligations upon the Contracting Parties to pursue a certain policy which will lead to the progressive realisation of these rights. The fact that it was more than a decade after the adoption of the European Convention before agreement was reached on the contents of the Charter is a clear indication of the problems which were encountered in the course of drafting. One of those problems was uncertainty as to the extent and substance of the obligations. It was not so much that the provisions in themselves were vague, but that the obligations based upon them were far from fixed. It was because this category of rights demands positive action, rather than non-interference, that governments were wary of committing themselves to the Charter.

4.2 Structure of the European Social Charter

The Charter consists of a preamble, five parts and an appendix. A number of substantive rights were added by way of the first Additional Protocol (1988). An Amending Protocol (1991) and a second Additional Protocol (1995) have been adopted in order to improve the Charter's supervisory machinery.

The preambles of the Convention and the Charter are similar in that both recall the aim of the Council of Europe as being the achievement of greater unity between its members through 'the maintenance and further realization of human rights and fundamental freedoms'. In the Charter's preamble, however, the importance of economic and social rights is less specified than that of civil and political rights in the preamble of the Convention. The former states simply that the Contracting Parties are resolved to make every effort to improve the standard of living and to promote the social well-being of their populations 'by means of appropriate institutions and action'.

Part I enumerates 19 principles which the Contracting Parties accept as their policy aims. This section does not lead to specific legal obligations. Part II includes substantive provisions on the right to work; the right to just conditions of work; the right to safe and healthy working conditions; the right to fair remuneration; the right to organise; the right to bargain collectively; the right of children and young persons to protection; the right of employed women to protection; the right to vocational guidance and training; the right to protection of health; the right to social security; the right to social and medical assistance; the right to benefit from social welfare services; the right of physically or mentally disabled persons to vocational training, rehabilitation and social resettlement; the right of the family to social, legal and economic protection; the right of mothers and children to social and economic protection; the right to engage in a gainful occupation in the territory of other Contracting Parties; and the right of migrant workers and their families to protection and assistance.[67]

Part III sets out the undertakings of the Contracting Parties[68] which, upon ratification of the Charter, do not have to accept the whole of Part II as long as they adopt not less than ten articles or 45 numbered paragraphs, including five of the seven key articles.[69] Part IV describes the supervision procedure, which will be examined below.[70] Part V contains the final provisions on derogations, restrictions, territorial application, etc.

The Appendix, which forms an integral part of the Charter, contains a number of so-called 'clarifications' on certain provisions of the Charter. They have been included at the insistence of governments which wanted more clarity on the scope of their obligations. This is another indication of States' insecurity as to the exact extent of their Charter obligations.

Unfortunately, these clarifications do not always serve their function. For example: Art 6(4) ESC recognises the right to collective action, including the right to strike (which is one of the few self-executing provisions of the Charter). The exercise of this right, like that of other rights in the Charter, is not subject to any restrictions or limitations 'except such as are prescribed by law and are necessary in a democratic society for the protection of the rights and freedoms of others or for the protection of public interest, national security, public health, or morals'.[71] This kind of public order clause is customary in international treaties.[72] So far every-

---

[67] Arts 1–19 ESC.
[68] Art 20 ESC.
[69] I.e. Arts 1, 5, 6, 12, 13, 16 and 19.
[70] See section 4.4.2 below.
[71] Art 31 ESC.
[72] See e.g. para 2 of Arts 8–11 ECHR.

thing is clear: the States which accept Art 6(4) ESC recognise the right of employees and trade unions to take collective action, including the right to strike, which shall not be restricted except under the conditions and for the reasons set out in Art 31. Confusion arises when the clarification clause is taken into account. It provides that each Contracting Party may regulate the right to strike by law, provided that any further restrictions that this might place on the right to strike can be justified under the terms of Art 31. What further restrictions? Art 31 prohibits any further restrictions other than those 'prescribed by law and necessary etc'. This particular clause was inserted at the insistence of the German government in an attempt to safeguard the restrictive right to strike in Germany. It did not preclude repeated criticism by the Charter's Committee of Experts, which found this to be a violation of Art 6(4).[73]

The substantive provisions of the Charter show every sign of having been drafted in the 1950s. Not only have some provisions been overtaken by socio-economic developments (e.g. Art 3(3), which stipulates a minimum of two weeks' paid holiday), but provisions relating to workers' representation and equal treatment (as distinct from equal pay) are not included. In that sense, the Charter is woefully old-fashioned.

The first Additional Protocol (1988) enshrines some of these 'new' rights: the right to equal opportunities and equal treatment in employment without discrimination based on sex; the right of workers to information and consultation, and to take part in the determination and improvement of working conditions; and the right of elderly persons to social protection.[74] Since most of these rights had already been established within the framework of the International Labour Organisation and, as regards equal treatment, the European Community, the Protocol came somewhat late in the day. However, this was not true of the right of elderly persons to social protection. The Protocol was the first international instrument to define legally binding obligations in that regard.

Apart from its perhaps too carefully worded provisions to avoid strict obligations for Contracting Parties, the principal weakness of the European Social Charter has always been its supervisory sys-

---

[73] See the reports on the Conclusions of the Committee of Experts, which are published at regular intervals.
[74] Arts 1–4 of the first Additional Protocol.

tem.[75] The weakness of the system is probably one of the main reasons for the Charter's low profile. In an attempt to reassert it as an important European human rights instrument, the control procedure was modified in 1991.[76] Further improvement is expected through the introduction of a collective complaints procedure.[77]

To date, however, the Charter has not succeeded in establishing itself as part of a European Bill of Rights to which people and States refer in their quest for improved living and working conditions. That role is generally reserved for the ILO; the specific European function having been superseded, to some extent, by the develoment of the social dimension of the European Community.

4.3 The revised European Social Charter

With the European Community moving further into the field of social rights, it was soon realised that the first Additional Protocol would not fulfil its role and that a complete overhaul of the Charter was necessary. In 1996 a revised Charter was adopted. It brings together in a single instrument the rights guaranteed by the original Charter and the first Additional Protocol, along with a number of new rights.[78] The revised Charter has the same structure as the old one.

More interesting are the new rights which have been inserted, in particular in relation to recent developments within the European Community. The new rights are set out in Arts 24–31. They include the right to termination of employment; the right of workers to protect their claims in the event of insolvency of the employer; the right to dignity at work; the right of workers with family responsibilities to equal opportunities and equal treatment; the right of workers' representatives to protection in undertakings; the right to information and consultation in collective redundancy procedures; the right to protection against poverty and social exclusion; and the right to housing. However, all these rights, apart from the right to housing, have been addressed for some time by both the ILO and the European Community. Consequently, there is little

---

[75] See section 4.4.2 below.
[76] See section 4.5 below.
[77] See section 4.6 below.
[78] By November 1997, 13 States (Belgium, Cyprus, Denmark, Finland, France, Greece, Italy, Lithuania, Portugal, Romania, Slovenia, Sweden and the United Kingdom) had signed the revised Charter. Some have indicated their intention to ratify it in the near future.

hope that this revision will enable the Council of Europe to regain a dominant position in the protection of economic and social rights.

In any case, the problem for the Charter is to gain, rather than to regain, a position as an important instrument of social progress in Europe. The Council of Europe itself has tended to treat the Charter as the proverbial stepchild. Even in simple matters like the housing of its committees, remuneration of committee members and publication of documents, the European Convention on Human Rights has always been treated much more favourably than the European Social Charter. It is only fairly recently that the *per diem* of members of the Committee of Experts has been raised to the same level as that of members of the Convention's Commission. Until recently, the Secretariat was tucked away in the periphery of the Council of Europe building in Strasbourg. When the European Convention's institutions moved to a new building, the Charter's Secretariat moved with them – to the basement of the building. The unequal treatment of the two instruments in these practical details is indicative of the Charter's inferior status even within the Council of Europe itself.

Some people thought that the recent adherence of eastern European States to the Council of Europe might give the Charter a second chance. Indeed, some of those States have readily signed the Charter. However, ratification is a different matter. At one time the argument in the Polish Parliament, for instance, was that accession to the ESC would be too expensive in that they could not afford to take all the measures necessary to fulfil their obligations under it. That was a rather weak argument as Poland had ratified a large number of ILO Conventions, most of which cover similar obligations and involve similar expense (if any). Besides, the new Member States attach more importance to accession to the Convention which, in their eyes, will establish them as democratic countries which respect the rule of law. The next, much more difficult, step for them will be to join the European Union. Accession to the Charter receives much less attention and support.

4.4 Scope and effect

4.4.1 Personal and territorial scope

By November 1997 twenty-one Council of Europe Member States had ratified the original Charter: all European Union Member

States plus Cyprus, Iceland, Malta, Norway, Poland and Romania. It applies to the metropolitan territories of the Contracting Parties and, if they notify the Secretary-General of the Council of Europe, also to their non-metropolitan territories.[79]

Unlike the European Convention, the rights in the Charter do not apply to every person within the territory of the Contracting Parties. According to the first section of the Appendix, the Charter applies to 'foreigners only insofar as they are nationals of other Contracting Parties lawfully residing or working regularly within the territory of the Contracting Party concerned'. Nationals of other countries do not have to be treated in the same way; foreigners who are recognised as refugees must be given 'treatment as favourable as possible'. Although this provision is based on the traditional international law principle of reciprocity, it creates interesting questions in the context of the non-discrimination principle in other treaties. For instance, how is this provision to be reconciled with Art 26 of the ICCPR, which states that all persons are equal before the law? Another principle of international law applies here: where there are two differing provisions, the more favourable one applies. In other words, if a State is bound by two conflicting provisions or provisions having different strengths, the more favourable (from the individual's point of view) applies. In the case of the Charter, this means that since the Charter clashes with Art 26 ICCPR, the Charter cannot be given effect, at least not in those Contracting Parties which are bound by the ICCPR.

4.4.2 Effect of the Charter in domestic law; control mechanism

Unlike the provisions of the Convention, those of the Charter cannot be invoked by individuals in their national courts or before an international body. There are a few possible exceptions to this, but they do not affect the general principle. Perhaps the only example of a Charter provision having self-executing effect is Art 6(4) (the right to strike), in the domestic legal order of the Netherlands.[80]

The absence of a right for individuals or non-governmental organisations to petition national or international bodies is probably the main reason why the Charter has been largely ignored over the last 35 years. While increasing use has been made of the Conven-

---

[79] Art 34 ESC.
[80] Supreme Court (*Hoge Raad*), 30 May 1986, *Nederlandse Jurisprudentie* 1986, 688.

tion's individual complaints system, thereby publicising the role and function of the Convention in the promotion of human rights protection in Europe, the lack of a complaints system has made the Charter an ineffective and therefore uninteresting instrument for the individual.

The Charter's supervisory mechanism consists of a reporting procedure.[81] Reports must be submitted by Contracting Parties on a regular basis. They are examined by the Commitee of Independent Experts[82] and subsequently by the Committee of Governmental Representatives and the Parliamentary Assembly. The reports and comments of all these bodies come together before the Committee of Ministers which issues recommendations to Contracting Parties which fail to comply with the Charter's requirements.

The procedure is a mixture of quasi-judicial and political supervision. Its main weakness is that the final word comes from a political body, which until 1993 failed to issue any recommendations. The reasons for this are partly political, partly technical. Politicians are usually reluctant to criticise each other for fear that they will be the subject of criticism. Moreover, the Committee of Ministers consists of a representative of every Council of Europe Member State, including any which have not ratified the Charter. Under the original Charter, the Committee has to adopt recommendations by a two-thirds majority of its members, while for many years the Charter's Contracting Parties represented about one-third of the Council of Europe's membership. It would be odd for a State which is not a party to the Charter to condemn practices in a State which has committed itself to fulfilling the Charter's obligations.

Other problems were caused by antagonism between the Committee of Experts and the Committee of Governmental Representatives which, for years, rejected the Experts' conclusions; and the lack of involvement of trade unions' and employers' organisations. Those bodies play a minor role in that they (that is, the international confederations of trade unions and employers' organisations) can sit as observers at the meetings of the Committee of Governmental representatives.[83] The national trade unions'

---

81 Arts 21–29 ESC.
82 See Lenia Samuel, *Fundamental Social Rights: Case law of the European Social Charter* (Council of Europe, 1997).
83 Art 27(2) ESC.

and employers' organisations also have the right to comment on the national reports.[84] Although there is no explicit provision to the effect that their comments shall be taken into account by the supervisory bodies, in practice they are taken into consideration. This minor role for employers' and workers' representatives is another reason for the Charter's lack of popularity. Employers' organisations and trade unions have focused their attention on the instruments of the ILO, in the framework of which they are involved in the drafting of standards as well as in the supervision of their implementation. With the development of social dialogue in the context of the European Community, the European federations of workers and employers directed their energies at influencing the Community's social policy. In an attempt to overcome the weaknesses of the Charter's supervisory system, a new procedure was established by the 1991 Amending Protocol.

4.5 The new supervisory procedure

The 1991 Protocol modifies a number of the Charter's provisions and significantly improves the control procedure. First of all, it enables the Committee of Experts to make direct contact with Contracting Parties in order to request clarifications and additional information concerning their reports.[85] Under the original provisions, the Experts could only conclude that certain situations were unclear and, therefore, that they were not sure whether the Charter had been infringed. They would then have to wait another two years to get the relevant information, which might still be inconclusive.

The second major improvement is that the task of the Governmental Committee is better defined.[86] This should avoid what happened previously, namely that the Governmental representatives more or less repeated the work of the Experts and, usually, came to different conclusions. This offered the Committee of Ministers an opportunity to abstain from any further action, as there was no clear indication of a breach of the Charter. The amendment provides that, in the light of the reports of the Experts and of the Contracting Parties, the Governmental Committee shall select the

---

84 Art 23 ESC.
85 Art 2 of the Protocol, amending Art 24 ESC.
86 Art 4 of the Protocol, amending Art 27 ESC.

situations which should, in its view, be the subject of recommendations by the Committee of Ministers.

A third step forward is the change in the voting procedure in the Committee of Ministers. The latter now adopts recommendations by a two-thirds majority of the Contracting Parties,[87] so Council of Europe Member States which have not ratified the Charter no longer have a vote. This should avoid some of the problems described above.

The Protocol will enter into force when all Contracting Parties to the Charter have expressed their consent to be bound by it, which is not yet the case.[88] Following a request by the Committee of Ministers, however, the supervisory bodies have applied the new procedure since the twelfth supervisory cycle (1989–1990),[89] which produced recommendations to Greece, Norway and the United Kingdom. The recommendations to Greece concerned the length of the compulsory period of service for career officers; penal sanctions against seamen in cases not involving the safety of the vessel; and the right to appeal in cases of (inadequate) medical assistance.[90] The recommendations to Norway concerned the right to collective industrial action[91] and the right of young children to the full benefit of compulsory education.[92] Those addressed to the United Kingdom concerned the right to collective industrial action[93] and inadequate maternity leave provisions.[94] The former related to legislation allowing employers to dismiss all employees taking part in strikes and to re-hire those workers on a selective basis up to three months after their dismissal. The criticism with regard to maternity leave related to the level of maternity benefits, which was considered to be too low in some cases.

---

87 Art 5 of the Protocol, amending Art 28 ESC.
88 By November 1997, only Austria, Cyprus, Finland, France, Greece, Ireland, Italy, Malta, the Netherlands, Norway, Poland, Portugal and Sweden had ratified the Protocol.
89 See International Journal of Comparative Labour Law and Industrial Relations, Selected Case Law, Summer 1994, p 147.
90 Art 1(2) and Art 13(1) and (4) ESC.
91 Art 6(4) ESC.
92 Art 7(3) ESC.
93 Art 6(4) ESC.
94 Art 8(1) ESC.

4.6 A system of collective complaints

In 1995, in a further attempt to improve the effectiveness of the Charter, a second Additional Protocol was adopted. This provides for a system of collective complaints. It will enter into force when five Member States of the Council of Europe have expressed their consent to be bound by it.[95] The Protocol is expected to enter into force in 1998.[96]

According to Art 1 of the Protocol, the Contracting Parties recognise the right of specified international organisations of employers and workers,[97] non-governmental organisations (NGOs) which have consultative status with the Council of Europe[98] and representative national organisations of employers and workers to submit complaints alleging 'unsatisfactory application' of the Charter.

Art 2 enables the Contracting Parties to allow other national NGOs with particular competence in the matters governed by the Charter to lodge complaints against them. Arts 3–10 set out the procedure to be followed. Complaints will be examined by the Committee of Independent Experts, which will decide on admissibility and merits. That Committee will send a report of its findings to the Committee of Ministers. The report will also be transmitted to the Parliamentary Assembly. If the Experts conclude that the Charter has not been applied in a satisfactory manner, the Ministers may adopt a recommendation (by a two-thirds majority of Contracting Parties) addressed to the State concerned. That State must provide information in the next supervisory cycle on the measures which it has taken to give effect to the recommendation.

4.7 The future of the European Social Charter

Although the adoption of these Protocols signals some progress as far as the effectiveness of the Charter is concerned, there is little

95 By November 1997, only Cyprus, Italy and Norway had done so. A further seven States had signed the Protocol.
96 For an excellent assessment, see David Harris, *The Collective Compaints Protocol to the European Social Charter*, Council of Europe, *The Social Charter of the 21st Century*, Colloquy in Strasbourg, 14–16 May 1997 (Doc SCColl/reple).
97 At present, the two recognised organisations are the European Confederation of Employers (UNICE) and the European Trade Union Congress (ETUC).
98 A list of eligible NGOs will be drafted by the Committee of Governmental Representatives.

evidence that it has gained in popularity. The Charter continues to operate very much in the shadow of the ILO and the European Community, which have been much more effective in their efforts to improve the standard of living of the populations of their Member States. The reluctance of most eastern European States to ratify the Charter may prove to be the last straw. If this situation remains unchanged, it will only underline the Charter's insignificance.

One way in which the Council of Europe could raise its profile with regard to the protection of economic and social rights would be by establishing a much closer link between civil and political rights and economic and social rights. One option would be to transfer some of the Charter's provisions (if necessary, after redefinition) to the Convention. This could be done with, for instance, the rights to organisation, collective bargaining and strike, the right to equal treatment in employment and certain aspects of worker participation rights. If such rights were given the same status as other rights in the Convention, they could be invoked in national courts and ultimately brought before the European Court of Human Rights, which could be given a 'Social Chamber'.

There remains the question of what should be done with those rights which are not easily translated into adversarially justiciable rights. If they were to remain in the Charter, the governments of the Contracting Parties would have to maintain their reporting obligation, but it is doubtful whether much notice would be taken of that. The time may have come for the Council of Europe to consider whether the protection of social rights in Europe is best served by an instrument which, since its adoption, has suffered badly from a near total lack of interest on the part of the people for whom it exists.

CHAPTER THREE

Human rights protection in the European Union

I. Introduction

The three European organisations established in the aftermath of the Second World War (OEEC,[1] the Council of Europe and the European Communities) sought to combat two major problems: complete economic downfall and the aftermath of one of the most vicious attacks on the dignity of humanity.

Whereas the Council of Europe focused on the protection of human rights, fundamental freedoms and democratic values, the OECD and the European Communities were concerned with the economic restoration of Europe. This was to be achieved through close co-operation of States, with a view to avoiding economic excuses for future inhumanity.

This separation of foci was one of the main reasons why human rights were not included in the foundation treaties of the European Communities. The protection of human rights was not entirely overlooked by the drafters of the treaties. There was some discussion as to whether or not to include certain provisions to this effect, but the idea was rejected. On the one hand, it was thought that the Council of Europe would take care of human rights. On the other, it was believed that the process of economic integration set forth in the Community Treaties could not lead to a violation of human rights. Consequently, none of the three foundation Treaties contained provisions on the protection of human rights.

Below, we examine the action undertaken by Community institutions to remedy the lack of express provisions concerning the protection of human rights, which has led to a firm commitment

[1] Now OECD.

to the development of such protection by the European Court of Justice (hereafter ECJ or the Court). In this chapter we discuss the cases which are landmarks in the development of the 'praetorial protection' of human rights in Community law.

2. The early case law of the Court of Justice

Shortly after the establishment of the Communities, it became clear that the ECJ would be called upon to protect human rights in the application of Community law. The first cases occurred under the Coal and Steel Treaty. In a number of mainly German and Italian cases, the Court was asked to decide whether or not certain Community acts violated the rights of Member States' citizens. At first, the Court refused to rule on this issue: its task was simply to interpret the Treaty and rule on the validity of Community instruments, and there was nothing on human rights in the Treaty. The Court explained the reasons for its passive attitude in *Stork*,[2] *Geitling*[3] and *Sgarlata*.[4]

The Stork company claimed that certain fundamental rights protected by the German Constitution had been violated by a decision of the High Authority[5] based on Art 65 ECSC. The Court held, first, that the High Authority was only required to apply Community law. It was not competent to apply national law. Similarly, under Art 31 of the ECSC Treaty, the Court was only required to ensure that, in the interpretation and application of the Treaty, the law was observed. It could not normally rule on provisions of national law. Consequently, the High Authority could not examine complaints of infringements of principles of German constitutional law.

The *Geitling* case dealt with the legality of decisions taken by the High Authority, which authorised joint buying and selling agreements in coal. The applicants claimed that the High Authority's decisions violated Art 14 of the German Constitution (the right to enjoyment of private property). Again, the Court rejected that argument. It held that it could not examine whether national law, even constitutional law, had been respected. It could 'neither

---

2   Case 1/58 [1959] ECR 17.
3   Joined Cases 36–38 and 40/59 [1960] ECR 423.
4   Case 40/64 [1965] ECR 215.
5   The predecessor of the Commission in the ECSC.

interpret nor apply'[6] national law in examining the legality of a decision of the High Authority. To make absolutely sure that everybody understood, the Court added that Community law 'does not contain any general principle, express or otherwise, guaranteeing the maintenance of vested rights'.[7]

In *Sgarlata*, a number of Italian citrus fruit producers sought to challenge a Community Regulation which fixed the price of citrus fruits. They objected that a restrictive interpretation of Art 173(2) EEC (which governed standing) would deprive them 'of all protection by the courts both under Community law and under national law, which would be contrary to the fundamental principles governing all the Member States'.[8] However, the Court held that 'these considerations . . . cannot be allowed to overrule the clearly restrictive wording of Art 173, which it is the Court's task to apply'.[9] Accordingly, the application was rejected because the applicants were not directly and individually concerned by the Regulation, which they had to be in order to challenge it before the ECJ.

Of particular interest in this case is the opinion of Advocate General Roemer, who observed that the applicants' argument of insufficient legal protection could have validity only if it were established that the Treaty guaranteed direct and complete legal protection to private individuals. Unless that were the case, the Court could do nothing about it since it could not amend the Treaty.

Another case which did nothing to ease the discomfort of all concerned with the protection of human rights was one which, as such, had nothing to do with human rights. It was, of course, *Costa v ENEL*,[10] in which the Court established the supremacy of Community law. When, in *Simmenthal*,[11] the Court added that Community law also prevailed over national constitutional law, the problem became acute, particularly in view of the ECJ's earlier decision that Community law could have direct effect.[12]

Indeed, if Community law was supreme over national law and if Community law did not protect human rights, who would protect human rights as expressly provided for in the constitutions of

6 Loc cit, at p 438.
7 Ibid, at p 439.
8 Loc cit, at p 227.
9 Ibid.
10 Case 6/64 [1964] ECR 585.
11 Case 92/78 *Simmenthal v Commission* [1979] ECR 777.
12 Case 26/62 *Van Gend en Loos* [1963] ECR 1.

the six original Member States? If national courts could not override Community law and the ECJ could not apply national law, where were individuals to go if, in the course of the application of Community law, their constitutionally guaranteed human rights were violated? The answer was: nowhere, unless the ECJ changed its course. Which it did, in *Stauder* v *City of Ulm*.[13]

3. Stauder v City of Ulm

Erich Stauder was entitled to buy Community butter at a reduced price. In order to prove their eligibility, applicants had to show that they were beneficiaries under certain social welfare schemes. According to some language versions of the relevant Decision, they had to identify themselves by any possible means, while other versions (including the German text) required them to give their name. Mr Stauder objected to having to disclose his name, claiming that this infringed his fundamental rights under the German Constitution.

The ECJ held that in the event of differing linguistic versions of a Community act, the most liberal interpretation must prevail provided that it achieves the act's objectives. Interpreted in this way, i.e. identification without giving name, there was nothing in the provision at issue which was 'capable of prejudicing the fundamental rights enshrined in the general principles of Community law and protected by the Court'.[14] So, whereas in previous cases the Court had denied all existence of human rights principles in Community law, it had now found the way to interpret human rights into the Treaty: they are enshrined in the general principles of Community law. As such, they are part of 'the law' which Art 164 TEC requires to be observed 'in the interpretation and application of this Treaty'.

3.1 Human rights and general principles of (Community) law

The Court's judgment in *Stauder* begged the question of whether general principles of Community law were any different from

---

13 Case 29/69 [1969] ECR 419.
14 Ibid, para 7.

other general principles of law. In other words, was this a new category of general principles of law which enshrined human rights?

The first question has never been answered because, in subsequent cases, the Court dropped the word 'Community'; it referred instead to 'general principles of law'. More intriguing is the question of the function of general principles of law as embracing human rights. Generally speaking, human rights are expressly laid down in a constitutional text (at national level) or in a treaty (at international level). They have a value of their own. They are not included in the far vaguer category of general principles of law, which do not necessarily have to be written down. They function as a standard of good behaviour of, usually, public authorities or governments. So, for instance, it is a general principle of law that abuse or misuse of power (*détournement de pouvoir*) is prohibited; it is a general principle that decisions of a public authority should be proportionate, or that people should be able to rely on the law (the principle of legal certainty). These well-established general principles of law are not the same as human rights. In Chapter 1 we pointed out that, as far as classic human rights are concerned, these create an area of freedom for the individual which has to be respected by public authorities. The above-mentioned general principles create binding standards of behaviour for public authorities so that the human rights of individuals are not endangered.[15]

It is not entirely clear why human rights, which form a clear category of their own, should be enshrined among these general principles. However, it is clear why the Court chose this formula. It was forced to find a way of recognising human rights through unwritten Community law. As suggested above, general principles of law usually form part of unwritten law. No legal order functions without such principles. In effect, they enabled the Court to introduce human rights protection in Community law. As we shall see, at first the Court did not incorporate the rights as such into the Community legal order. It merely stated that respect for fundamental (human) rights formed an integral part of the general principles of law protected by the Court of Justice.

---

[15] Some authors do not draw this distinction. See e.g. John Temple Lang, 'The sphere in which Member States are obliged to comply with the general principles of law and Community fundamental rights principles', Legal Issues of European Integration, 1991/2, p 23.

4. The post-*Stauder* period

Since its judgment in *Stauder*, the ECJ has not looked back. It has been called upon time and again to pronounce on the protection of human rights in Community law. Although it is now recognised that the Court has established itself as a protector of human rights, its earlier case law is not without inconsistency. That is because the Court had to find a way of establishing a firm basis for human rights protection, without so much as a reference to this in the foundation Treaties.

In the next section we survey the development of human rights protection in the Court's case law, beginning with *Internationale Handelsgesellschaft*. This is the famous case in which the German Federal Constitutional Court (*Bundesverfassungsgericht*) made it clear that it would refuse to accept the ECJ's ruling that national courts could not set aside Community law, if the Community rule violated the constitutional rights of German citizens. The Constitutional Court's stance in this case has had much wider significance than in the area of human rights protection. Its judgment had and still has great significance for the existence of the Communities as such.

4.1 The ECJ's case law on human rights protection in Community law

Internationale Handelsgesellschaft[16] was the first post-*Stauder* human rights case. The issue was whether a Community Regulation which established a deposit system for exporters was consistent with principles in the German Constitution. At stake were the principles of freedom of action and of disposition, of economic liberty and proportionality. A German court had refused to apply the deposit system because of the alleged violation of those constitutional principles. While reiterating that it could not examine national (constitutional) law, the ECJ observed that respect for human rights forms an integral part of the general principles of law. It added that '[t]he protection of such rights, whilst inspired by the constitutional traditions common to the Member States, must be ensured within the framework of the structure and objectives of the Community'.[17]

16 Case 11/70 [1970] ECR 1125.
17 Ibid at p 1134, paras 3–4.

In *Nold*,[18] the Court not only referred again to 'common constitutional traditions' as a source of inspiration, but also turned for the first time to international human rights treaties 'on which the Member States have collaborated or of which they are signatories'.[19] The question was whether a Commission Decision which prevented Nold from buying coal directly from the selling agency violated principles of German constitutional law. Although in later cases it became clear that the Court was thinking of the European Convention on Human Rights in particular, it did not mention that instrument explicitly here. The applicant had specifically referred to the ECHR, but the Court did not follow suit.

In *Rutili*,[20] however, the ECJ referred to specific articles of the European Convention which it said could provide guidelines for human rights protection in the Community legal order. The issue was the freedom of movement of Mr Rutili, an Italian employed in France who was ordered to move to another *département* because of his participation in trade union activities in Meurthe-et-Moselle. The Court used specific provisions of the Convention as guidelines for the interpretation of the public policy limitations on the freedom of movement as laid down in Art 48(3) EEC. It regarded those limitations as a specific manifestation of the more general principle enshrined in Arts 8–11 ECHR and Art 2 of Protocol No 4 to the Convention, which provide that 'no restrictions in the interests of national security or public safety shall be placed on the rights secured by the above-mentioned articles other than such as are necessary for the protection of those interests in a democratic society'.[21]

An appeal to specific provisions of the ECHR does not necessarily guarantee success, however. In *Prais*[22], the applicant invoked the freedom of religion, which is one of the rights protected in Art 9 ECHR. She wanted to participate in a competition for a post at the Council which was to be held on the first day of *Shavuot* (Pentecost). The Jewish religion forbade her to travel on that day. Unfortunately, Ms Prais had failed to inform the Council of this when she applied; she only did so three weeks before the competition was due to take place. The Court held that although an appointing

---

18 Case 4/73 *Nold* v *Commission of the European Communities* [1974] ECR 491.
19 Ibid, para 13.
20 Case 36/75 *Rutili* v *Minister for the Interior* [1975] ECR 1219.
21 Ibid, para 32.
22 Case 130/75 *Prais* v *Council of the European Communities* [1976] ECR 1589.

authority should inform itself of the days which for religious reasons might be unsuitable for competitions, 'neither the Staff Regulations nor the fundamental rights already referred to can be considered as imposing a duty . . . to avoid a conflict with a religious requirement of which the authority has not been informed'.[23]

In *Hauer*,[24] the ECJ acknowledged the siginificance of the Convention but did not decide the case on that basis. Liselotte Hauer was refused permission to plant vines on her property because of a Council Regulation. She claimed that her right to property and her right to pursue freely a trade or profession, both guaranteed by the German constitution, were violated. The ECJ examined the Regulation's validity in the light of Community law, including the protection of human rights. It considered that its acceptance of the ECHR as a source of human rights protection in Community law had been recognised by the Communities' political institutions, as evidenced by the Joint Declaration of 5 April 1977.[25] It saw this recognition as confirmation of its human rights case law.

With regard to the right to property, the Court referred to Protocol No 1 to the ECHR. Finding insufficient guidance there, however, it turned to constitutional principles, in particular those expressed in the German, Italian and Irish constitutions. From that examination it concluded that the social function of the right to property could result in a restriction of its enjoyment. The second question was whether the restrictions imposed by the Regulation were disproportionate and an intolerable interference with the right. The ECJ decided that the restriction on the use of property was justified by objectives of general interest pursued by the Community and did not infringe the right to property in the form in which it is protected in the Community legal order.[26]

In *National Panasonic*,[27] the action of Community officials was challenged. They had arrived unannounced at the company's premises in order to investigate its books. National Panasonic alleged that there had been a violation of the right to respect for private and family life, home and correspondence laid down in Art 8 ECHR which, it argued, applied *mutatis mutandis* to legal persons. The Court did not respond to that argument, focusing instead on

---

23 Ibid, para 18.
24 Case 44/79 *Hauer v Land Rheinland Pfalz* [1979] ECR 3727.
25 OJ 1977 C 103/1.
26 Loc cit, para 30.
27 Case 136/79 *National Panasonic v Commission* [1980] ECR 2033.

the limitation clause in Art 8(2) ECHR. That provision allows interference with the exercise of the rights in Art 8(1) only in so far as such interference is necessary in a democratic society in the interests of national security, public safety or the economic well-being of the country, for the prevention of disorder or crime, etc. According to the ECJ, the power of the Commission to carry out investigations without prior notification was justified by the need to avoid a distortion of competition to the detriment of the public interest, individual undertakings and consumers.[28]

Since those early cases, the Court of Justice has examined the relevance for Community law of many specific provisions of the European Convention. While it relies particularly on the Convention, it has also occasionally referred to other international treaties, such as ILO Convention No 111 on discrimination in respect of employment and occupation[29] and the European Social Charter.[30]

Many cases have involved a review of Community instruments in the light of human rights protection. The Court has consistently held that the Community institutions are bound by human rights. To that extent the protection of human rights is guaranteed within the Community legal order, but the same cannot be said of the European Union as a whole. For all practical purposes the ECJ currently has no jurisdiction over activities which fall within the spheres of common foreign and security policy (CFSP) and co-operation in the fields of justice and home affairs (CJHA). The Court itself has drawn attention to the fact that legal problems may arise because of the denial of judicial protection to individuals affected by the Union's activities, especially in the context of CJHA.[31] Pending the entry into force of the Amsterdam Treaty, CJHA is essentially intergovernmental and any complaint of an infringement of the Convention would have to be brought (if possible) before the courts of the Member State or States directly involved and thereafter to Strasbourg.[32] As we shall see in Chapter

---

28 Ibid, para 20.
29 Case 149/77 *Defrenne* v *Sabena* (*No 3*) [1978] ECR 1365.
30 Ibid. See also Case 24/86 *Blaizot* v *University of Liège* [1988] ECR 379.
31 *Report of the Court of Justice on Certain Aspects of the Application of the Treaty on European Union*, Proceedings of the Court of Justice and Court of First Instance of the European Communities, No 15/95, p 5 (hereafter *Report of the Court of Justice*).
32 A M Arnull, 'Opinion 2/94 and its implications for the future Constitution of the Union', in University of Cambridge Centre for European Legal Studies, *The Human Rights Opinion of the ECJ and its Constitutional Implications*, CELS Occasional Paper No 1, p 8.

7, however, under the Amsterdam Treaty a large part of CJHA will become subject to Community rules and ECJ jurisdiction. Without doubt, the ECJ has put human rights protection firmly on the European Communities' agenda. From scratch, that is without any explicit reference to human rights in the foundation Treaties, the Court has built up its case law, incorporating the protection of human rights first on the basis of general principles of law and then increasingly on the basis of the European Convention on Human Rights. Having begun by acknowledging that the Convention 'can supply guidelines which should be followed within the framework of Community law' (*Nold*), the Court has strengthened the Convention's impact by recognising it as a direct source of Community law. The turning point was the adoption in 1986 of the Single European Act, which expressed the Member States' determination 'to work together to promote democracy on the basis of the fundamental rights recognised in the Convention'.[33] In *Commission* v *Germany*,[34] for example, the ECJ held that the requirement of respect for family life set out in Art 8 ECHR is recognised by Community law.

Nevertheless, so far the Court has used the Convention only as a source of human rights protection; that is, to help determine the content of general principles of law. It has not stated that a particular provision of the ECHR forms part of Community law. That this is not accidental became clear when the Court was asked whether the Community could accede to the Convention without the need for a treaty amendment. The Court's response to that question will be discussed in Chapter 5.

4.2 Human rights as a constraint upon Community institutions as employers

In general terms, the ECJ has stated that '[i]n the exercise of its present jurisdiction, the Court already examines whether fundamental rights have been respected by the legislative and executive authorities of the Communities'.[35] More precisely, 'respect for human rights is a condition of the lawfulness of Community acts'.[36] In this section we consider two cases which demonstrate

---

33 SEA Preamble, third recital.
34 Case 249/86 [1989] ECR 1263.
35 *Report of the Court of Justice*, para 20.
36 Opinion 2/94 [1996] ECR I-1759, para 34.

that the institutions must respect human rights not only when they act in their political capacity, but also as employers.[37]

In *Maurissen and European Public Service Union v Court of Auditors*,[38] the ECJ annulled a decision by the Court of Auditors for breach of human rights. It held:

> the freedom of trade union activity ... means not only that officials and servants have the right without hindrance to form associations of their own choosing but also that such associations are free to do anything lawful to protect the interests of their members as employees.

> It thus follows, in the first place, that the Community institutions and bodies may not prohibit their officials and servants from joining a trade union or staff association or from participating in trade union activities, or impose any penalty whatsoever on them by reason of such membership or activities.

> It also follows that the Community institutions and bodies must allow trade unions and staff associations to fulfil their proper role, *inter alia* by keeping officials and servants informed, representing them *vis-à-vis* the institutions and other bodies and participating in consultations with those institutions and bodies on all matters affecting staff, and may not treat them differently without justification.[39]

Similarly, upholding an appeal against a decision of the Court of First Instance in *X v Commission*,[40] the ECJ annulled a Commission decision refusing to employ the appellant for lack of physical fitness, on the grounds that his right to respect for his private life had been infringed: he had been subjected to an Aids test without his consent. Nevertheless, it confirmed that a person's rights may be restricted provided that the restrictions correspond to objectives of general public interest and do not constitute a disproportionate and intolerable interference with the very substance of the right protected.[41]

That proviso may be at odds with the European Convention, which stipulates that restrictions (where permitted) must be 'pres-

---

37 See also *Prais*, loc cit, note 22.
38 Joined Cases C-193 and 194/87 [1990] ECR I-95.
39 Ibid, paras 13–15.
40 Case C-404/92P [1994] ECR I-4737.
41 Ibid, para 18.

cribed by law' and 'necessary in a democratic society'[42] and exhaustively identifies the interests which may justify such a restriction.[43] If so, it tends to undermine the claim that the ECJ has never knowingly disregarded a relevant provision of the Convention or refused to follow the case law of the Strasbourg Court,[44] and raises the question of the relationship between the two European Courts. These problems are discussed further in Chapter 6.

5. The 'Solange' cases

The above-mentioned *Internationale Handelsgesellschaft* case[45] led to a 'revolution' by the German Federal Constitutional Court (*Bundesverfassungsgericht*), the consequences of which are still felt today. A lower German court had referred to the ECJ the question of the validity of certain provisions of a Regulation which allegedly violated principles enshrined in the German Constitution. The referring court observed that, although Community regulations are not national laws, they must respect the fundamental rights guaranteed by the German Constitution. However, the ECJ held that recourse to national law in order to determine the validity of Community acts would have an adverse effect on the uniformity and efficacy of Community law. The validity of Community rules can be judged only in the light of Community law. Such validity cannot be affected by allegations that it runs counter to fundamental rights as formulated by the Constitution of a Member State. The Court went on to declare that respect for fundamental rights forms an integral part of the general principles of law.[46]

While this was an important step towards the establishment of human rights protection within the Community, the ECJ's judgment provoked an angry reaction on the part of the German Constitutional Court. Having received the ECJ's answer to its preliminary question, the lower court stayed the proceedings and referred the case to the Constitutional Court, asking more or less

---

42 See e.g. Arts 8(2), 9(2), 10(2) and 11(2) ECHR.
43 See P van Dijk, *Judicial Protection of Human Rights in the European Union – Divergence, Cordination, Integration*, Exeter Paper in European Law No 1 (1986), p 8, n 27.
44 Arnull, op cit, p 8.
45 Loc cit, note 16.
46 Ibid, paras 3–4.

the same question: did the Community Regulation violate German constitutional law and, if so, what would the Constitutional Court do about it? Was it not up to that Court to review the constitutionality of Community law in the context of the German legal system?

The Constitutional Court observed that the case demanded clarification of the relationship between secondary Community law and the guarantees of fundamental rights in German constitutional law.[47] It agreed with the ECJ that Community law constitutes an independent system of law flowing from an autonomous source. However, although the Constitutional Court could not rule on the validity or otherwise of a rule of Community law, it could declare such a rule to be inapplicable in Germany if fundamental rights were violated.[48] It was its task to protect German citizens' fundamental rights as guaranteed by the Constitution and no court could deprive it of that duty. In short, the ECJ determines the validity of Community law and the Constitutional Court decides on the compatibility of Community law with German constitutional law.

The Constitutional Court stated that fundamental rights form an inalienable feature of the German Constitution. It warned that it would control the compatibility of Community law with those rights so long as the Community lacked: (a) a democratic parliament directly elected by general suffrage to which the Community's legislative organs are fully responsible; and (b) a codified catalogue of fundamental rights, the substance of which is reliably and unambiguously fixed for the future in the same way as the substance of the Constitution. It said that legal certainty could not be guaranteed merely by decisions of the ECJ.[49] Hence, this is generally known as the *Solange* ('so long as') case; *Solange I* to be precise, because the *Bundesverfassungsgericht* would temper the effect of its judgment somewhat in *Solange II*.[50]

The reaction in Community circles to *Solange I* was one of horror, because the *Bundesverfassungsgericht* threatened to undermine the uniform interpretation and application of Community law on which the operation of the common market depends. In its

---

[47] *Internationale Handelsgesellschaft mbH* v *Einfuhr- und Vorratsstelle für Getreide und Futtermittel* [1974] 2 CMLR 540.
[48] Ibid, para 28.
[49] Ibid, para 23.
[50] See below.

judgment, the Constitutional Court had said that it would not apply Community law if it was incompatible with fundamental rights as guaranteed by the German Constitution.[51] The particularly worrying aspect was that it made no distinction between primary and secondary Community law. This first serious threat to the supremacy of Community law led to a flurry of declarations and assurances that the Community really did take human rights seriously.

The Constitutional Court modified its position in July 1979, following certain political and legal developments in the Community. The European Parliament had just been directly elected for the first time, in 1977 the Community's principal political institutions had declared that they would respect human rights[52] and the ECJ's human rights case law was encouraging. Accordingly, in *Steinike*[53] the Constitutional Court now held that it could not declare inapplicable norms of primary Community law. However, it left open the question whether and, if so, to what extent, in view of those developments, the principles expressed in *Solange I* could continue 'to claim validity without limitation in respect of . . . norms of *derived* Community law'.[54]

That question was answered in *Solange II* in October 1986,[55] in the light of the Community's 'convincing advances' in the protection of human rights:

> so long as the European Communities, and in particular the case law of the European Court, generally ensure an effective protection of fundamental rights . . . the Federal Constitutional Court will no longer exercise its jurisdiction to decide on the applicability of secondary Community legislation . . . and will no longer review such · legislation by the standard of the fundamental rights contained in the Constitution.[56]

Seven years later, in its well-known *Maastricht* judgment,[57] the Constitutional Court warned that it would maintain 'an effective

---

51 Cf. the judgment of the Italian Constitutional Court in *Frontini v Ministero delle Finanze* [1974] 2 CMLR 372.
52 See note 25 above.
53 *FA Steinike und Weinling v Bundesamt für Ernährung und Forstwirschaft* [1980] 2 CMLR 531.
54 Ibid, para 12.
55 *Re the Application of Wünsche Handelsgesellschaft* [1987] 3 CMLR 225.
56 Ibid, para 48.
57 *Brunner v The European Union Treaty* [1994] 1 CMLR 57.

protection of basic rights for the inhabitants of Germany ... as against the sovereign powers of the Communities'. Nevertheless, it declared that it would exercise its jurisdiction on the applicability of secondary Community legislation in Germany in a 'relationship of co-operation' with the ECJ.[58]

Despite that conciliatory message, it seems that the German Constitutional Court remains prepared to declare Community law inapplicable if it infringes human rights. This became apparent in the context of the recent *Banana* cases, which concerned a Community Regulation on the common organisation of the market in bananas.[59]

The important cases in the context of this book are those in which the German government and German operators on the banana market argued that the Regulation should be declared null and void. It was alleged that the Regulation was discriminatory and that it violated the right to property and the right to pursue a profession or business. The ECJ dismissed these complaints[60] and a German court subsequently rejected the operators' demands for relief. However, basing its ruling on the fundamental right to effective judicial protection guaranteed by the German Constitution, the Constitutional Court ordered the lower court to re-examine the case. In the course of its re-examination, that court granted limited interim relief.[61]

Dissatisfied, the applicant began proceedings against the customs authorities seeking permission to import bananas without licences and free of customs duties.[62] Although the Constitutional Court dismissed his appeal for procedural reasons, it recognised that the national courts might suspend the application of the Regulation temporarily in summary proceedings because of the presentation of new arguments.[63] Subsequently, the highest German financial court (*Bundesfinanzhof*) questioned the applicability of the Regulation despite the ECJ's earlier ruling on validity, on the grounds that it could be seen as an instance of the Community's

58 Ibid, para 13.
59 See U Everling, 'Will Europe slip on bananas? The Bananas judgment of the Court of Justice and national courts' (1996) 33 CMLRev 401.
60 Case C-280/93 *Germany* v *EU Council* [1994] ECR I-4973; Case C-286/93 *Atlanta* v *Council and Commission* (21 June 1994).
61 Everling, op cit, p 431.
62 Ibid.
63 Judgment of 26 April 1995. Ibid, p 432.

exceeding its competence – another reason for the non-application of Community law in Germany as expressed by the Constitutional Court in its *Maastricht* judgment.[64]

These decisions by the highest German courts represent a direct challenge to the supremacy of Community law. They threaten the fundamental principle of uniform application on which the common market rests. The issue has been dealt with here because it illustrates the importance of effective human rights protection in Community law. The *Bundesverfassungsgericht* and the *Bundesfinanzhof* are obviously not satisfied with the way things stand. They want a much clearer indication as to which human rights are protected in Community law.

6. Political developments

The message in *Solange I* was clear: the Community suffers from a democratic deficit, one element of which is the lack of express provisions with regard to the protection of human rights in the Community legal order.

In 1976, the Commission submitted its first report on this matter to the European Parliament and the Council.[65] It discussed the question of whether the Communities should accede to the European Convention on Human Rights. The Commission concluded that accession was unnecessary, since the norms of the Convention were already generally binding in Community law. No further constitutive act was needed to achieve this.[66] The Commission based its opinion on the Court's judgment in *Nold*,[67] clearly overlooking the careful wording of the Court, which merely acknowledged that international treaties like the Convention 'can supply guidelines'. It would be several years before the Court adopted a more definite formula.[68]

While the Commission considered the situation with regard to the protection of human rights in Community law to be satisfactory, it observed that the position would be strengthened if the Community's political institutions were to declare their respect for

---

64 Loc cit, note 57.
65 Report of the Commission of 4 February 1976, EC Bulletin, Supplement 5/76.
66 Ibid, at p 14.
67 Loc cit, note 18.
68 See section 4.1 above.

human rights. That occurred in 1977, when the Commission, Council and European Parliament published a non-binding declaration to that effect.[69] Although the Commission promised to pursue its efforts to safeguard and extend the freedom of the individual citizen, it did not say how this would be achieved. A Citizens' Europe was still a long way off.

The European Parliament was less than satisfied with the Commission's 1976 report and urged a follow-up study. This came three years later when, in a famous memorandum,[70] the Commission changed its mind. It now favoured the Communities' accession to the European Convention on Human Rights. Although the Commission maintained its view that human rights protection, as ensured by the ECJ, was satisfactory, it recognised that legal certainty was lacking: the individual did not know in advance which rights would and which would not be recognised by the Court. The need for a written catalogue of human rights was acknowledged.

In its enthusiasm, spurred on by the *Bundesverfassungsgericht*, the Commission made light of the obstacles to accession by a community of States which lacked many characteristics of a democratic State order. The Commission was aware that its preferred solution would exclude social rights, and it recognised that the best way of protecting human rights in the Community was by adopting a comprehensive Bill of Rights. However, accession to the ECHR was seen as a quicker solution. Drafting a Community Bill of Rights would take much longer, since agreement would have to be reached on all its definitions. That would be difficult, particularly with regard to economic and social rights.[71]

All the same, Community accession to the European Convention has still not been achieved. In 1994 the ECJ was asked for an opinion on the legal aspects of accession. It concluded that there would have to be a formal amendment of the EC Treaty on the basis of Article 236, which requires unanimity among the Member States.[72] The obstacles are political rather than legal. Formally, progress has been limited to recognition of the Convention in the

---

[69] See note 25.
[70] *Accession of the Communities to the European Convention for the Protection of Human Rights and Fundamental Freedoms*, 4 April 1979, EC Bulletin, Supplement 2/79.
[71] Ibid, at p 5.
[72] See Chapter 5.

Single European Act, the Maastricht Treaty and the Amsterdam Treaty.[73] For its part, however, attaching special significance to the Convention, the Court has quietly developed an impressive body of case law on the protection of human rights in Community law.

7. The role of economic and social rights

As seen above, the focus throughout has been on civil and political rights. As in other international contexts, economic and social rights were considered to be more difficult to define and thus to protect. The difference between the European Community and other international organisations is, however, that the Community is (or was) mainly an economic organisation, which makes the protection of economic and social rights at least as relevant as the protection of civil and political rights.

The attitude towards social rights was sharply reversed in the 1980s. Unofficial reports suggested that the President of the Commission, Jacques Delors, wanted to be the architect of a European Bill of Rights, exactly 200 years after the adoption of the French *Déclaration des Droits de l'Homme et du Citoyen*. The truth of these rumours cannot be vouched for, but the fact is that in 1989 the Community Charter of Fundamental Social Rights for Workers was adopted. It should be added that the social dimension of the Community was high on the European Council's agenda at that time, as demonstrated by the declarations at the end of the 1988 summits in Hannover and Rhodes, which emphasised the importance of creating a solid social dimension to the internal market.

The Commission started the procedure for drafting the Community Charter by asking the European Parliament and the Economic and Social Committee for their opinions on a Community Bill of Basic Social Rights. Compared to developments with regard to civil and political rights, it took, contrary to the Commission's view in 1979, a relatively short time to agree on the social rights to be protected in Community law.

Two observations should be made here. First, the Member States were not unanimous, as the then British Prime Minister, Margaret Thatcher, was opposed to such a Charter. At the 1997

---

73 See Chapter 7.

Amsterdam summit, however, the new British government committed itself to signing the Community Charter. Secondly, the Charter is a non-binding political declaration without legal effect. Hence, it cannot be enforced as such. It provides for a reporting procedure whereby the Commission publishes an annual report on the implementation of the Charter.[74] Although reporting procedures can be quite useful in detecting problems and monitoring developments, this particular procedure is weakened by the three principles on the basis of which it operates: respect for the principle of subsidiarity, respect for the diversity of national systems and preservation of business competitiveness ('having regard to the need to reconcile economic and social considerations'). The latter principle, in particular, is inconsistent with the fundamental character of human rights.

Another development which should be mentioned here is the inclusion of a reference to the European Social Charter in the preamble of the Single European Act.[75] The reference to the ESC mysteriously disappeared from the Maastricht Treaty, only to reappear in the recent Amsterdam Treaty.[76]

7.1 The relationship between the two European Charters

The existence of two European Charters on social rights (three if we include the revised ESC adopted in 1995)[77] promotes confusion, particularly among politicians and the media. They call the Community Charter the 'Social Charter' or even the 'European Social Charter', which is an entirely different instrument. In terms of substance, legal nature and effect, the two instruments are very different.

In the first place, the European Social Charter (ESC) is an intergovernmental treaty, adopted in 1961 within the framework of the Council of Europe. It creates legally binding obligations for its Contracting Parties.[78] In contrast, the Community Charter of Fundamental Social Rights for Workers is a political declaration of intent by the Heads of State or Government of the Member States, which creates no legally binding obligations for the Community in-

---

[74] Para 29 of the Community Charter.
[75] See text at note 33 above.
[76] See Chapter 7.
[77] See Chapter 2, section 4.3.
[78] See Chapter 2, section 4.

stitutions or for the Member States themselves. In the words of Jacques Delors, the Community Charter is meant to discover how far the Member States have recognised common values and how these can be 'illustrated in rights'.[79] To that end, the Commission publishes an annual report.

The two Charters also differ widely in the rights included. A number of rights appear only in the European Social Charter: the rights to work; reasonable daily working hours; additional paid holidays and reduced working hours for persons engaged in dangerous or unhealthy occupations; remuneration for overtime; a reasonable term of notice for termination of employment; medical control for young employees; special protection for children and young persons; maternity leave; nursing infants; night and underground work of women; vocational guidance; protection of health; social security and social assistance; social welfare services; social, legal and economic protection for families; social and economic protection of mothers and children.

The following provisions appear only in the Community Charter: freedom of movement; approximation of living and working conditions; development of certain aspects of employment regulations; the obligation to stipulate employment conditions; freedom not to join a professional organisation or trade union; obligation to allow collective agreements at European level.

In spite of their different wording, some provisions focus on the same issues: 'development of certain aspects of employment regulations' (Community Charter) could refer to quite a number of the more specific provisions of the European Social Charter. Some provisions are common to both Charters, such as the freedom of association and the right to free collective bargaining. However, only the Community Charter recognises the so-called 'negative' freedom of association, i.e. the freedom *not* to join a trade union. This freedom, which relates to the issue of closed shops, was left out of the European Social Charter because the United Kingdom still had closed shop practices with which the international bodies did not want to interfere. Interestingly, the Court of Human Rights has now held that Art 11(1) ECHR encompasses a negative right of association, even though such a right had been intentionally excluded from the Convention.[80]

---

[79] In a speech to the Parliamentary Assembly of the Council of Europe, October 1989. Council of Europe, Parl Ass AS/SOC (41)21, p 2.

[80] *Sigurjonsson* v *Iceland* (A/264) (1993) 16 EHRR 462.

The co-existence of the two Charters does not create legal problems. Their content and effect differ to such an extent that they do not hamper each other's style in legal terms. In political terms, however, the adoption of the Community Charter was a severe blow to the European Social Charter, which the Council of Europe regards as Europe's social constitution. The Community Charter has played an important role in the formulation of Community social legislation in the 1990s, especially in the first half of this decade. All instruments, including the Maastricht Agreement on Social Policy, bear a reference to it. Of course, the Community Charter itself constitutes 'soft law', since it lacks legal force.

The central question at this point must be why the European Social Charter was not incorporated into the body of Community law and why, indeed, the Commission did not propose that the Communities should adhere to the European Social Charter as it did with regard to the European Convention on Human Rights.[81] Suffice to say that there was little support for such a step because the ESC was not considered to be the right instrument for the Community. A specific Community instrument was preferred, even one lacking legal force. The most recent proposal by a so-called *Comité des Sages* is to include a list of human rights in the Treaty on European Union, in which a number of civil and political as well as economic and social rights are included.[82]

---

[81] See Chapter 6.
[82] *For a Europe of Civic and Social Rights* (Brussels, 1996). For the text, see L Betten and D MacDevitt, *The Protection of Fundamental Social Rights in the European Union* (Kluwer Law International, 1996), p 241. See also Chapter 7.

CHAPTER FOUR

The domestic implications of the ECJ's human rights case law

I. Introduction

In the previous Chapter we established that 'respect for human rights is a condition of the lawfulness of Community acts'.[1] As an integral part of the general principles of Community law, however, human rights also constrain the authorities of the Member States whenever they act 'within the framework of Community law'. At the very least, this means that whenever a Member State implements, derogates from or otherwise applies Community rules, it must act in conformity with human rights. It follows that, in such circumstances, the ECJ is competent to entertain questions concerning the compatibility of national legislation with the European Convention on Human Rights.

2. Human rights as a contraint upon the Member States

The fact that human rights constrain the Member States as well as the Community institutions has long been apparent from the ECJ's case law. Besides highlighting the European Convention as a source of general principles to which it will have recourse, for example, the Court's judgment in *Rutili*[2] implied that provisions of Community law must be construed and applied by Member States with reference to the rights enshrined in the Convention. Some

---

1   Opinion 2/94 *Accession by the Community to the Convention for the Protection of Human Rights and Fundamental Freedoms* [1996] ECR I-1759, para 34.
2   Case 36/75 [1975] ECR 1219. See Chapter 3, section 4.1.

years later, in *Kirk*,[3] the United Kingdom found itself constrained (albeit indirectly) by the principle that penal provisions cannot be retroactive, which is embodied in Art 7 of the Convention.

Kirk concerned a dispute over the validity of British regulations prohibiting Danish vessels from fishing within the United Kingdom's 12-mile fishery zone. Art 100 of the 1972 Act of Accession had authorised the United Kingdom to restrict fishing by other Member States' nationals until 31 December 1982. Following the Council's failure to adopt Community provisions for the conservation and management of fishery resources after that date, the Commission declared that Member States could adopt national conservation measures subject to its approval. The United Kingdom's Sea Fish Order 1982 was approved by the Commission on 5 January 1983. The following day, Captain Kirk, a Danish skipper, was arrested for unlawful fishing. He was fined £30,000 and appealed to the Crown Court, which requested a preliminary ruling by the ECJ. The retroactivity point arose because the United Kingdom and the Commission argued that the Sea Fish Order was sanctioned by a Council Regulation of 25 January 1983, which authorised retroactively (as from 1 January 1983) the retention of national measures derogating from the Community principle of non-discrimination on grounds of nationality. Acknowledging that the prohibition of retroactive penal provisions constitutes a human right, the ECJ held that the Regulation could not validate '*ex post facto* national measures of a penal nature which impose penalties for an act which, in fact, was not punishable at the time at which it was committed'.[4]

The Court of Justice clearly has no jurisdiction to examine the compatibility with the Convention of national rules which lie outside the scope of Community law.[5] This was recently confirmed in *Kremzow*,[6] a case which illustrates the point well. A retired Austrian judge was found guilty of murdering an Austrian lawyer and sentenced to 20 years' imprisonment. The appeal court upheld his conviction. In 1993, however, the Court of Human Rights found a violation of Art 6(3)(c) of the European Convention, since the

3 Case 63/83 R v *Kirk* [1984] ECR 2689.
4 Ibid, para 22.
5 *See* Joined Cases 60 and 61/84 *Cinéthèque* [1985] ECR 2605; Case 12/86 *Demirel* [1987] ECR 3719; Case C-144/95 *Maurin* [1996] ECR I-2909.
6 Case C-299/95 *Kremzow v Austria* (29 May 1997)

appeal had been heard in Mr Kremzow's absence.[7] Mr Kremzow then brought a domestic action for damages for unlawful detention. He argued that, as a citizen of the EU, he enjoyed the right to free movement of persons under Art 8a TEC; and that a State which infringed that right by executing an unlawful penalty of imprisonment was liable in damages under Community law. The Supreme Court requested a preliminary ruling on the interpretation of Art 164 TEC and various provisions of the Convention.

The ECJ ruled that, since the relevant national legislation related to a situation which lay outside the scope of Community law, it could not give the interpretative guidance necessary for the national court to decide whether that legislation was in conformity with human rights. While any deprivation of liberty may impede the right to free movement, a purely hypothetical prospect of exercising that right does not establish a sufficient connection with Community law to justify the application of Community provisions. Moreover, the provisions of national law under which Mr Kremzow had been sentenced were not designed to secure compliance with rules of Community law.

The position is altogether different when a Member State acts within the framework of Community law, as the ECJ held in *ERT*:[8]

> On the other hand, where such [national] rules do fall within the scope of Community law, and reference is made to the Court for a preliminary ruling, it must provide all the criteria of interpretation needed by the national court to determine whether those rules are compatible with the fundamental rights the observance of which the Court ensures and which derive in particular from the ECHR.[9]

In *ERT*, a Greek court requested a preliminary ruling as to the compatibility with various provisions of the EEC Treaty and Art 10 ECHR (freedom of expression) of a national system of exclusive television rights. The ECJ held[10] that the monopoly was prohibited by Art 59 EEC (freedom to provide services) unless it could be justified on grounds of public policy, public security or public health.[11] Following the above paragraph, it continued:

7 *Kremzow v Austria* (A/268-B) (1994) 17 EHRR 322.
8 Case C-260/89 [1991] ECR I-2925.
9 Ibid, para 42.
10 Ibid, para 26.
11 See Arts 66 and 56 TEC.

In particular, when a Member State relies on the combined provisions of Articles 56 and 66 in order to justify rules which are likely to obstruct the exercise of the freedom to provide services, such justification, provided for by Community law, must be interpreted in the light of the general principles of law and in particular of fundamental rights. Thus the national rules in question can fall under the exceptions provided by the combined provisions of Articles 56 and 66 only if they are compatible with the fundamental rights the observance of which is ensured by the Court.[12]

ERT shows that when a Member State takes measures which restrict a Community freedom, those measures must respect human rights. National courts must always check compliance with human rights when assessing the legality of a governmental measure which restricts a freedom derived from the EC Treaty.

Such a measure was at issue in *Commission* v *Germany*.[13] German law prohibited individuals from importing medicines (available only on prescription in Germany) which were prescribed by a doctor and purchased at a pharmacy in another Member State, even where the quantities involved did not exceed normal personal needs. The ECJ found a violation of Art 30 EEC. Rejecting the German government's submission that the measure was saved by the 'public health' clause of Art 36, it held:[14]

The right of privacy and the right to the protection of medical secrets, which is one aspect of it, are fundamental rights protected by the Community legal system: see Case 136/79, *National Panasonic* v *EC Commission*.[15] As the Court held in [ERT], when a Member State relies on provisions of the Treaty to justify a national regulation which is likely to obstruct the exercise of a freedom guaranteed by the Treaty, such justification ... must be interpreted in the light of the general principles of law, particularly fundamental rights. However, such rights are not absolute privileges, but may be subject to restrictions, provided that the latter actually promote the objectives of general interest pursued by

---

[12] Loc cit, note 8, para 43. See also Case 5/88 *Wachauf* [1989] ECR 2609: Member States must respect human rights when implementing Community rules.
[13] Case C-62/90 [1992] ECR I-2575.
[14] Ibid, para 23.
[15] [1980] ECR 2033.

the Community and are not, by reference to such objective, disproportionate and intolerable to such an extent that they would interfere with the very substance of the rights thus safeguarded: Case 265/87, *Schräder*.[16] The protection of public health and the life of humans is one of the objectives likely to justify such restrictions.

While national authorities could check, for the purposes of the protection of public health, imports of medicinal products supplied only on prescription in the importing State, those checks had to be carried out in such a way as to meet the requirements arising from the protection of human rights. The German government had not shown that it was impossible to implement controls which would meet the requirements of the protection of public health without unduly impairing medical confidentiality.[17]

3. The domestic reach of general principles of Community law regarding the protection of human rights

The European Convention on Human Rights is not yet part of United Kingdom law.[18] However, since the ECJ uses the Convention as an aid to the construction of Community texts, s 3(1) of the European Communities Act 1972 requires British courts (if they do not request a preliminary ruling under Art 177 TEC) to determine the meaning or effect of Community provisions in the light of the Convention. Moreover, as an integral part of the general principles of law, the rights and freedoms enshrined in the Convention demand protection by British courts in all cases which are within the framework of Community law.

The domestic reach of the general principles of Community law was recently considered in *R v MAFF, ex parte First City Trading Ltd*,[19] where the High Court had to decide whether the legality of the Beef Stocks Transfer Scheme depended upon its compliance with the principle of equality. Relying upon the judgment in *Phil Collins*,[20] where the ECJ held that German copyright law was sub-

16 [1989] ECR 2237, para 15.   17 Loc cit, note 13, para 25.
18 See Chapter 7, section 4.
19 [1997] 1 CMLR 250.
20 Joined Cases C-92/92 and C-326/92 [1993] ECR I-5145.

ject to the principle of non-discrimination on grounds of nationality in Art 7 EEC[21] (because intellectual property rights are 'such as to affect trade in goods and services, and competition in the Community'[22]), counsel for the applicants argued that the legality of a national measure is subject to general principles of Community law if it affects intra-Community trade in goods or services. However, Laws J held that the general principles elaborated by the ECJ have a narrower reach than those articulated in the Treaty itself and that the former apply only to acts done in pursuance of Community law. His Lordship reasoned that the Treaty is superior to the law made by the ECJ, a court of limited jurisdiction:

> These fundamental principles ... are not provided for on the face of the Treaty of Rome. They have been developed by the Court of Justice ... out of the administrative law of the Member States. They are part of what may perhaps be called the common law of the Community. That being so, it is to my mind by no means self-evident that their contextual scope must be the same as that of Treaty provisions relating to discrimination or equal treatment, which are statute law taking effect according to their express terms . . . .
>
> Like any statute law containing orders or prohibitions, the Treaty is *dirigiste*; it is ... to be sharply distinguished from law which is made by a court of limited jurisdiction, such as the Court of Justice.
>
> The power of the Court of Justice ... to apply ... principles of public law which it had itself evolved cannot be deployed in a case where the measure in question, taken by a Member State, is not a function of Community law at all . . . . Where action is taken, albeit under domestic law, which falls within the scope of the Treaty's application, then of course the Court has the power and duty to require that the Treaty be adhered to. But no more: precisely because the fundamental principles elaborated by the Court of Justice are not vouchsafed by the Treaty, there is no legal space for their application to any measure or decision taken otherwise than in pursuance of Treaty rights or obligations.[23]

---

[21] Now Art 6 TEC (to be renumbered Art 12).
[22] *Loc cit*, note 20, para 22.
[23] *Loc cit*, note 19, paras 39–42.

However, such reasoning may be open to question. The general principles of Community law have not been 'made' by the ECJ. Rather, they are fundamental principles which the Court has discovered in the constitutional traditions common to the Member States and in certain human rights treaties. They belong to the very foundation of the Community's legal order, as Advocate General Dutheillet de Lamothe observed in *Internationale Handelsgesellschaft*:[24] 'the fundamental principles of national legal systems . . . contribute to forming that philosophical, political and legal substratum common to the Member States from which through the case-law an unwritten Community law emerges.'

As such, the domestic reach of those principles surely cannot be less extensive than that of principles which are enshrined in the Treaty. Indeed, the ECJ has recognised that principles articulated in the Treaty are merely specific manifestations of underlying general principles.[25] Accordingly, the general principles of Community law (including human rights) arguably apply to all national measures which have effects in an area covered by Community law,[26] whether or not such measures are adopted in pursuance of Community rights or obligations.

3.1 Do general principles regarding the protection of human rights have horizontal direct effect?

In *R v MAFF, ex parte Bostock*,[27] Advocate General Gulmann posed the following question:

> whether the Community law principles regarding the protection of fundamental rights may in some cases be relied on as creating obligations in proceedings between individuals and not just in proceedings between individuals and the authorities which are the primary addressees of fundamental rights.[28]

---

24 Case 11/70 [1970] ECR 1125 at 1146.
25 See e.g. Joined Cases 201 and 202/85 *Marthe Klensch v Secrétaire d'Etat à l'Agriculture et à la Viticulture* [1986] ECR 3477.
26 Cf. the opinion of Advocate General Van Gerven in Case C-159/90 *Society for the Protection of Unborn Children (SPUC) v Grogan* [1991] ECR I-4685 at 4723, para 31.
27 Case C-2/92 [1994] ECR I-955.
28 Ibid, at 975, para 39.

The force of the argument that human rights constitute objective values constraining public authorities and private parties alike is difficult to deny. Nevertheless, it is suggested that a negative response should be given to the question. The general principles concerned are essentially principles of public law, designed to protect individuals *vis-à-vis* public authorities (not only the Community authorities but also national authorities when they act within the framework of EC law). That is reflected in the principles' origin, the constitutional traditions common to the Member States and international human rights treaties which the Member States have signed or on which they have collaborated. Regarding the latter, it is significant that the European Convention on Human Rights does not impose obligations directly on individuals (although individuals are affected indirectly through such positive obligations as it imposes upon States).[29] The sole exception to the denial of horizontal direct effect, it is suggested, is where a general principle is enunciated in a Community instrument which is itself capable of having such effect. Thus, the principles of non-discrimination on grounds of nationality[30] and equal pay for equal work[31] have horizontal direct effect but only by virtue of the Treaty provisions by which they are mediated.

This conclusion is supported by ECJ case law. In *Defrenne* (No 3),[32] the applicant complained of sex discrimination with regard to working conditions. The Court acknowledged that non-discrimination on grounds of sex is one of the general principles of Community law. However, at the material time the Community had not 'assumed any responsibility for supervising and guaranteeing the observance of the principle of equality between men and women in working conditions other than remuneration'.[33] This was because the Equal Treatment Directive[34] had not entered into force. Ms Defrenne was unable to rely upon the general principle of equality alone. Subsequently, of course, the Directive ('simply the expression, in the relevant field, of the principle of equality')[35] came into force, but with vertical direct effect only.[36]

---

29 See e.g. *X and Y v Netherlands* (A/91) (1986) 8 EHRR 235. See further Harris, O'Boyle and Warbrick, *op cit*, pp 19–22.
30 Art 6 TEC (to be renumbered Art 12).
31 Art 119 EC (to be renumbered Art 141).
32 Case 149/77, [1978] ECR 1365.   33 Para 30.   34 76/207/EEC.
35 Case C-13/94 *P v S and Cornwall County Council* [1996] ECR I-2143, para 18.
36 Case 152/84 *Marshall v Southampton and South West Hampshire Area Health Authority (Teaching)* [1986] ECR 723.

Nevertheless, human rights may have indirect third-party effect through their influence upon the interpretation of domestic provisions. This is consistent with German law, for example.[37] It also reflects the Community law doctrine of 'consistent interpretation', according to which national courts must do everything possible to interpret provisions of national law in conformity with Community directives, which do not impose obligations directly upon individuals.[38]

4. Is judicial review an adequate remedy for the purpose of enforcing human rights?

The right to an effective remedy is guaranteed by Art 13 of the European Convention, which requires the provision of a domestic remedy allowing the competent national authority both to deal with the substance of the relevant Convention complaint and to grant appropriate relief.[39] In addition, Art 6 ECHR enshrines the right to a fair trial. This guarantees access to the courts for the protection of 'civil rights', a term which excludes matters relating exclusively to public law.[40]

Inspired partly by Arts 6 and 13 of the Convention, Community law guarantees full and effective judicial protection of all rights ('civil' or otherwise) deriving from provisions of Community law. In *Johnston* v *Chief Constable of the RUC*,[41] this meant that a certificate issued by the Secretary of State could not be conclusive evidence that derogation from the equality principle was justified, despite Art 53 of the Sex Discrimination (Northern Ireland) Order 1976. The applicant had been a member of the RUC full-time Reserve. It was common ground that the reason why her full-time

---

37 See N G Foster, *German Legal System & Laws* (Blackstone Press, 2nd edn, 1996), pp 155–6.
38 Case C-106/89 Marleasing [1990] ECR I-4135.
39 *Chahal* v *United Kingdom* (1997) 23 EHRR 413, para 145. However, the effectiveness of a remedy for the purposes of Art 13 does not depend upon the certainty of a favourable outcome for the applicant. See *Vilvarajah* v *United Kingdom* (A/215) (1992) 14 EHRR 248, para 122.
40 *Schouten and Meldrum* v *Netherlands* (A/304) (1995) 19 EHRR 432, para 50. See further the opinion of Advocate General Ruiz-Jarabo Colomer in Joined Cases C-65 and 111/95 R v *Secretary of State for the Home Department, ex parte Shingara* [1997] All ER (EC) 577.
41 Case 222/84 [1986] ECR 1651.

contract had not been renewed was the Chief Constable's decision not to employ women in the full-time Reserve; and that if she had been a man she would have been offered a new full-time contract. Mrs Johnston claimed to be a victim of sex discrimination. Before the Industrial Tribunal hearing, a 'conclusive evidence' certificate was issued by the Secretary of State, stating that the refusal to offer full-time employment to Mrs Johnston was for the purpose of safeguarding national security and protecting public safety and public order. However, the ECJ held that Art 6 of the Equal Treatment Directive stipulated a requirement of judicial control which underlies the constitutional traditions common to the Member States and is laid down in Arts 6 and 13 of the European Convention. By virtue of that requirement, 'all persons have the right to obtain an effective remedy in a competent court against measures which they consider to be contrary to the principle of equal treatment for men and women laid down in the directive'.[42]

In *Commission v Belgium*,[43] the ECJ described as one of the general principles of Community law:

> that any person must be able to obtain effective judicial review before the national courts of national decisions which may infringe a right conferred by the Treaties, and ... that principle requires that the persons concerned must be able to obtain from the administration, prior to their bringing any action, knowledge of the grounds of such decisions.[44]

Advocate General Tesauro summed the position up in his opinion in *Factortame (No 1)*:

> It is therefore firmly established, in the light of the Court's well-settled case-law, ... that national courts are required to afford complete and effective judicial protection to individuals on whom enforeceable legal rights are conferred under a directly effective Community provision ... and that from this it follows that any national provision or practice which precludes those courts from giving 'full effect' to the Community provision is incompatible with Community law.[45]

---

42 Ibid, para 19.
43 Case C-249/88 [1991] ECR I-1274.
44 Ibid, para 25. See also Case 222/86 *UNECTEF v Heylens* [1987] ECR 4097.
45 Case C-213/89 *R v Secretary of State for Transport, ex parte Factortame Ltd* [1990] ECR I-2433 at 2455, para 15.

Against this background, it is important to consider whether judicial review proceedings in English law constitute an effective remedy, particularly for the purpose of protecting rights conferred by Community law. In such proceedings, the court does not examine the merits of a decision as such but confines itself to considering whether the administrative authority acted illegally, unreasonably or unfairly.[46] The meaning of 'unreasonable' was recently explained as follows: 'Judicial review is not a forum for speculation or opinion as to whether the decision was right or wrong. To be quashed it has to be totally unreasonable: outrageous in its defiance of logic.'[47] Nevertheless, decisions which affect human rights are subjected to 'the most anxious scrutiny': .

> The court may not interfere with the exercise of an administrative discretion on substantial grounds save where the court is satisfied that the decision is unreasonable in the sense that it is beyond the range of responses open to a reasonable decision-maker. But in judging whether the decision-maker has exceeded this margin of appreciation the human rights context is important. The more substantial the interference with human rights, the more the court will require by way of justification before it is satisfied that the decision is reasonable in the sense outlined above.[48]

As far as the Court of Human Rights is concerned, the narrow limits of judicial review generally satisfy the Convention's requirements.[49] In *Bryan*,[50] which concerned the adequacy of proceedings to challenge an enforcement notice in the town and country planning context, the Court found no breach of Art 6(1) ECHR. It held that the High Court's limited power of review 'can reasonably be expected in specialised areas of law such as the one at issue' and 'is frequently a feature in the systems of judicial control of administrative decisions throughout the Council of Europe Member

---

[46] See e.g. *Council of Civil Service Unions v Minister for the Civil Service* [1985] AC 374.

[47] *R v Radio Authority, ex parte Bull* [1997] 2 All ER 561 at 577h (per Aldous LJ).

[48] *R v Ministry of Defence, ex parte Smith* [1996] QB 517 at 554E-G, *per* Sir Thomas Bingham MR. See also *R v Secretary of State for the Home Department, ex parte Launder* [1997] 1 WLR 839.

[49] For criticism of this approach, see M Hunt, *Using Human Rights Law in English Courts* (Hart Publishing, 1997), pp 315–19.

[50] *Bryan v United Kingdom* (1996) 21 EHRR 342.

States'.[51] Similarly, in *Soering*[52] and *Vilvarajah*[53] the Court considered judicial review proceedings to be an effective remedy for the purposes of Art 13 ECHR in relation to complaints raised under Art 3 in the contexts of deportation and extradition. Although the principle of proportionality is not yet recognised as a separate ground for review (save as required by Community law)[54] and judicial review does not permit scrutiny of the merits of an administrative decision, the Court was satisfied that English courts could control the legality of executive discretion on substantive and procedural grounds and quash decisions as appropriate.[55] In *Chahal*,[56] however, where national security considerations were invoked by the Secretary of State as grounds for deportation, judicial review was inadequate since it could not ensure independent scrutiny of the applicant's Art 3 claims. It was not enough for the domestic court to satisfy itself that the Minister had balanced the risk to the applicant against the danger to national security.[57]

The Strasbourg Court has been described as 'cautiously inhibited' in comparison with the Court of Justice.[58] Within the Community law framework, judicial review cannot be confined to examining whether there is illegality, irrationality or procedural impropriety. More extensive scrutiny is required in order to ensure the observance of limits laid down by Community law.[59] In particular, administrative action must be reviewed in the light of the general principles of Community law,[60] including human rights. The reviewing court must consider whether there is a breach of such principles as proportionality or legitimate expectation as understood and applied by the ECJ:

---

51 Ibid, para 47. See also *Fayed* v *United Kingdom* (A/249-B) (1994) 18 EHRR 393; *AGOSI* v *United Kingdom* (A/108) (1987) 9 EHRR 1; and *Air Canada* v *United Kingdom* (A/316) (1995) 20 EHRR 150. *Cf. W* v *United Kingdom* (A/121) (1988) 10 EHRR 29.

52 *Soering* v *United Kingdom* (A/161) (1989) 11 EHRR 439, paras 121–124.

53 Loc cit, note 40, para 123.

54 See below.

55 See also *D* v *United Kingdom* (1997) 24 EHRR 423.

56 Loc cit, note 39.

57 Ibid, paras 148–153.

58 Lord Lester of Herne Hill QC, *General Report*, 8th International Colloquy on the ECHR (Budapest, 20–23 September 1995), Council of Europe, pp 234–236.

59 Case 182/84 *Criminal proceedings against Miro BV* [1985] ECR 3731.

60 See further J A Usher, *General Principles of EC Law* (Longman, 1998).

In my view the national court may not automatically accept the view of the national legislature or limit itself to deciding whether the national legislature, in the light of the proportionality requirement, could reasonably have adopted the legislative provisions in question.[61]

Regarding legitimate expectation, substantive as well as procedural expectations must be protected.[62] In short, the scrutiny of national measures within the scope of Community law must be no less intensive than that of Community acts by the CFI and the ECJ under Art 173 TEC. This reflects the position regarding liability in damages. In respect of the conditions governing Member State liability in damages for breach of Community law, the ECJ has declared that such conditions 'cannot, in the absence of particular justification, differ from those governing the liability of the Community in like circumstances'.[63]

This raises the question whether, within the framework of Community law, domestic judicial review proceedings must involve a full right of appeal. That question has been referred to the ECJ by the Court of Appeal in *Upjohn*,[64] in the context of an application for judicial review of the Licensing Authority's decision to revoke a product licence under the Medicines Act 1968. Since the applicant in that case is relying on rights conferred by a Community Directive,[65] is the High Court required to review the merits of the Authority's decision, or is it limited to deciding whether the decision was one which the Authority could reasonably have reached? In the light of the Strasbourg Court's attitude towards judicial review, the ECJ could decide that a full right of appeal is not required. On the face of it, this would be consistent with *Shingara*,[66] which concerned the remedies available to EU nationals denied

61 Case C-306/88 *Rochdale Borough Council v Anders* [1992] ECR I-6458 at 6480 *per* Advocate General Van Gerven, who expressed the view that the limited judicial review exercised by Hoffmann J in *Stoke-on-Trent City Council v B & Q plc* [1991] WLR 42 conflicted with the ECJ's ruling in *Miro*.
62 See the cases cited in the judgment of Sedley J in *R v MAFF, ex parte Hamble Fisheries (Offshore) Ltd* [1995] 1 CMLR 533; *cf R v Secretary of State for the Home Department, ex parte Hargreaves* [1997] 1 All ER 397.
63 See Joined Cases C-46 and 48/93 *Brasserie du Pêcheur and Factortame (No 3)* [1996] ECR I-1029, para 42.
64 Case C-120/97 *Upjohn Ltd v Licensing Authority established by the Medicines Act 1968*. See OJ 1997 No C 142/15.
65 Directive 65/65/EEC.
66 Joined Cases C-65 and 111/95 *R v Secretary of State for the Home Department, ex parte Shingara* [1997] All ER (EC) 577.

entry to the United Kingdom for reasons of public policy. There, the ECJ considered judicial review proceedings to be sufficient for the purposes of Art 8 of Directive 64/221/EEC, which guarantees persons refused entry 'the same legal remedies . . . as are available to nationals of the State concerned in respect of acts of the administration'. However, we should not read too much into the Court's judgment in *Shingara*. The ECJ was not asked to consider the effectiveness of judicial review as such, but whether nationals of other Member States refused entry to the United Kingdom on grounds of public policy were entitled to the same remedy as UK nationals (i.e. an appeal to an immigration adjudicator). The Court based its decision on the different substantive rights of a State's own nationals, who cannot be denied access to the national territory, and the corresponding need to allow the competent national authorities a margin of discretion in the application of the public policy proviso to other EU nationals.[67] Accordingly, *Shingara* does not resolve the question of the effectiveness of judicial review as a means of protecting rights conferred by Community law.

On that question of principle, the conclusions of Advocate General Ruiz-Jarabo Colomer in *Shingara* are compelling. Observing that 'the Court of Justice has raised the right of citizens to judicial protection to the status of an essential guarantee within the Community legal order',[68] he opined that Community law requires 'an effective remedy which ensures that the entire administrative decision, including its substantive grounds, is subjected to judicial scrutiny'.[69] This would enhance the protection of rights conferred by Community law and ensure parity of judicial protection for individuals within the Community legal order. There can be no justification for subjecting acts to different levels of judicial scrutiny depending on whether they are adopted by the Community or by a Member State. As Advocate General Tesauro observed in *Brasserie du Pêcheur* and *Factortame (No 3)*:

> In a Community governed by the rule of law, in which it is the aim that the acts and conduct of all participants in the system should be amenable to judicial review without privileges for anyone, the requirement of effective protection of the rights claimed by individuals under Community law may not vary –

---

67 Ibid, para 30 of the judgment.
68 [1997] All ER (EC) 577 at 593, para 75.
69 Ibid, at 601, para 131.

given equal situations – depending on whether a Member State or the Community caused the loss or damage.[70]

Whilst such a development would have serious consequences for administrative law-making and judicial review in the United Kingdom, it cannot be ruled out on that ground. In application of the principle of co-operation laid down in Art 5 of the EC Treaty, national courts must be prepared to create new remedies if that is necessary in order to ensure the effective protection of Community rights.[71] Nevertheless, the intensity of judicial review would vary according to the context of the proceedings, as it does in cases before the ECJ. This was recognised by Steyn LJ (as he then was) in relation to the Community principle of proportionality in *R v Secretary of State for the Home Department, ex parte Adams*:[72]

> As English judges it seems to us that explanations of that principle span a spectrum of views from a narrow doctrine not essentially very different from *Wednesbury* unreasonableness to a *de novo* review of the administrative decision . . . . Even in respect of proportionality there may be a margin of appreciation. And it is not self-evident that the principle of proportionality may not need to be adapted to the special circumstances of a case involving a tension between freedom of speech and national security.[73]

For example, according to the ECJ's long-established case law on the judicial review of Community acts in cases involving the evaluation of a complex economic situation, such as the implementation of the Common Agricultural Policy, the Court confines itself to examining whether the exercise of discretion contains a manifest error, or constitutes a misuse of power or whether the institution has clearly exceeded the bounds of its discretion.[74]

Similar flexibility is evident under the European Convention. In *Klass*[75] and *Leander*,[76] for example, the Strasbourg Court held that Art 13 required a remedy which was 'as effective as can be' in circumstances where national security considerations did not permit

---

70 [1996] ECR I-1029 at 1104, para 68.
71 Case C-213/89 *R v Secretary of State for Transport, ex parte Factortame Ltd (No 1)* [1990] ECR I-2433.
72 [1995] All ER (EC) 177.
73 Ibid, at 192.
74 See e.g. Case 138/79 *Roquette Frères v Council* [1980] ECR 3333 at 3358, para 25.
75 *Klass v Germany* (A/28) (1979) 2 EHRR 214.
76 *Leander v Sweden* (A/116) (1987) 9 EHRR 433.

the disclosure of certain sensitive information. However, it should be noted that those cases concerned complaints under Arts 8 and 10 ECHR.[77] In *Chahal*,[78] the Court observed that the requirement of a remedy which is 'as effective as can be' is not sufficient in respect of a complaint that deportation will expose a person to a real risk of treatment in breach of Art 3,[79] where national security issues are immaterial. In such cases, given the importance attached to Art 3 and the irreversible nature of the harm which might occur if the risk materialised, the notion of an effective remedy requires independent scrutiny of the applicant's claim that there are substantial grounds for fearing a real risk of ill-treatment, without regard to any perceived threat to the security of the expelling State.[80]

---

77 The right to respect for private and family life and the right to freedom of expression, respectively.
78 Loc cit, note 39.
79 Prohibition of torture and of inhuman or degrading treatment or punishment.
80 *Chahal, loc cit*, paras 150–151.

CHAPTER FIVE

The relevance of ECHR provisions and case law to EU lawyers

1. Introduction

Given the status of the rights and freedoms enshrined in the European Convention on Human Rights within the Community legal order, this chapter will consider the implications of the Convention's provisions and case law for the interpretation and application of EU law. For the purpose of illustrating the Convention's relevance to EU lawyers, we have chosen six themes on account of their social and economic importance and especially their close relationship to the operation of the common market. However, it should be noted that what follows is by no means an exhaustive survey of the EU law–ECHR interface or of the legal issues to which the themes give rise.

2. Freedom of movement

The free movement of persons is one of the EC Treaty's fundamental objectives.[1] In his opinion in *Konstantinidis*[2] Advocate General Jacobs expressed the view that a person who relies on Arts 48, 52 or 59 of the Treaty in connection with employment or an occupation in another Member State is 'entitled to assume that, wherever he goes to earn his living in the European Community, he will be treated in accordance with a common code of fundamental values,

---

1 See *Report of the High Level Panel on the free movement of persons chaired by Mrs Simone Veil*, presented to the Commission on 18 March 1997 (hereafter *Report of the High Level Panel*).
2 Case C-168/91 [1993] ECR I-1191.

in particular those laid down in the European Convention on Human Rights.'[3] The right to freedom of movement is no longer restricted to people who are economically active. Art 8a(1) TEC provides that 'Every citizen of the Union[4] shall have the right to move and reside freely within the territory of the Member States, subject to the limitations and conditions laid down by this Treaty and by the measures adopted to give it effect'. According to the ECJ, however, citizenship of the Union is not intended to extend the scope *ratione materiae* of the Treaty to internal situations which have no link with Community law.[5] A purely hypothetical prospect of exercising a Community freedom does not suffice.[6] This means that the right to freedom of movement cannot be relied upon with regard to situations which are purely internal to a Member State.

For example, *R v Saunders*[7] concerned a British national who pleaded guilty to theft and was bound over in return for an undertaking to return to Northern Ireland and stay out of England and Wales for three years. The undertaking was broken and the question was whether the court order violated the Treaty's free movement provisions. The ECJ found no violation. It held that the application by a court in a Member State to a national of that State of a measure restricting the person's freedom of movement within the State as a penal measure provided for by national law by reason of acts committed within the State was a wholly domestic situation which fell outside the scope of the Treaty. Similarly, in *Steen (No 1)*,[8] a person who had never exercised his right to freedom of movement within the Community could not rely on Arts 7[9] and 48 of the Treaty against his own Member State in relation to the conditions affecting his recruitment to a post in that State's territory.[10]

In contrast, Art 2(1) of Protocol No 4 to the European Convention provides that 'Everyone lawfully within the territory of a State

---

3 Ibid, para 46. In Case C-2/92 *R v MAFF, ex parte Bostock* [1994] ECR I-955, however, Advocate General Gulmann considered this 'too far-reaching'.
4 Art 8(1) provides: 'Every person holding the nationality of a Member State shall be a citizen of the Union.'
5 See e.g. Joined Cases C-64 and 65/96 *Land Nordrhein-Westfalen v Kari Uecker and Vera Jacquet v Land Nordrhein-Westfalen* [1997] 3 CMLR 963.
6 Case C-299/95 *Kremzow v Austria* (29 May 1997).
7 Case C-175/78 [1979] ECR 1729.
8 Case C-332/90 [1992] ECR I-341.
9 Prohibition of discrimination on grounds on nationality (now Art 6 TEC).
10 See further Case C-132/93 *Steen (No 2)* [1994] ECR I-2715.

shall, within that territory, have the right to liberty of movement and freedom to choose his residence'. Being enshrined in the Convention system, the right to liberty of movement within a State is protected as part of the general principles of Community law. This is because the ECJ draws inspiration from international human rights treaties on which the Member States have collaborated or of which they are signatories.[11] All EU Member States except Greece have signed Protocol No 4, and Greece was a member of the Council of Europe when the Protocol was concluded in 1963. Arguably, therefore, Art 2(1) should influence the interpretation and application of the EC Treaty. Nevertheless, it is doubtful whether this will persuade the ECJ to alter its conclusion that the Community right to freedom of movement does not apply in 'wholly internal' situations.

The applicability of Art 8a(1) TEC in such situations was one of the questions referred to the ECJ for a preliminary ruling in *Adams*, where the President of Sinn Fein challenged an order prohibiting him from entering Great Britain and thus preventing him from attending a political meeting at the House of Commons.[12] In the context of freedom of movement within the EU, that case also raised the important issue of the impact of national security interests upon the freedom of speech, which is protected by Art 10(1) ECHR. In particular, did the exclusion order constitute a disproportionate interference with the applicant's rights as an EU citizen? Since the reference was withdrawn following the order's revocation, no ruling was delivered by the ECJ and no judgment given by the High Court. Nevertheless, it is interesting to consider what the outcome might have been. If the measure in question had been found to restrict Mr Adams' Community law rights, it would have had to be assessed in the light of Convention standards.[13] Art 10(2) ECHR permits restrictions on the freedom of speech which are 'necessary in a democratic society, in the interests of national security', States being afforded a margin of appreciation in matters of national security.[14] However, they 'may not, in the name of the struggle against terrorism, adopt whatever measures they deem ap-

---

[11] See Chapter 3. Art 2 of Protocol No 4 was referred to in Case 36/75 *Rutili* [1975] ECR 1219.

[12] *R v Secretary of State for the Home Department, ex parte Adams* [1995] All ER (EC) 177.

[13] See Chapter 4.

[14] See *Hadjianastassiou* v *Greece* (A/252-A) (1992) 16 EHRR 219.

propriate.'[15] Moreover, Strasbourg case law shows that the most careful scrutiny is required when freedom of political debate by opposition politicians is restricted, since 'free political debate is at the very core of the concept of a democratic society.'[16] Against this background, even allowing for the special problems involved in combating terrorism, it is arguable that the exclusion order would have been declared unlawful, involving, as it did, an absolute prior restraint on political debate.

Unlike EU citizens, third-country nationals lawfully within the Union enjoy the Community right to freedom of movement and residence only if they have an appropriate link with Community law, for example, through marriage to a Union citizen.[17] Art 2(1) of Protocol No 4 confers upon them no such entitlement because it is not a direct source of Community rights and obligations. Thus, in *Sevince*,[18] which concerned the Dutch authorities' refusal to extend a Turkish national's residence permit, Advocate General Darmon concluded that Art 2 did not support the view that residence without the permit required by national law was lawful. Nevertheless, the expulsion of a third-country national from the territory of a Member State, for example on the dissolution of marriage to an EU citizen,[19] must be consistent with Convention standards. In particular, expulsion may give rise to an issue under Art 3 of the Convention, thus engaging the responsibility of the expelling State, where substantial grounds are shown for believing that the person would face a real risk of suffering torture or inhuman or degrading treatment in the receiving country. In such circumstances, Art 3 implies the obligation not to expel the person to that country.[20] In any case, Art 8 of the Convention, which guarantees the right to respect for family life, supports the argument that Community law should recognise a right of residence for a third-country national who is the divorced spouse of a Union citizen, especially if there are children of the marriage.[21]

---

15 *Klass v Germany* (A/28) 2 EHRR 214, para 49.
16 *Castells v Spain* (A/236) (1992) 14 EHRR 445, para 43.
17 *Report of the High Level Panel*, Chapter VI.
18 Case C-192/89 *Sevince v Staatssecretaris van Justitie* [1990] ECR I-3461.
19 See Case 267/83 *Diatta v Land Berlin* [1985] ECR 567.
20 See e.g. *Chahal v United Kingdom* (1997) 23 EHRR 413, para 74.
21 *Report of the High Level Panel*, pp 74–5. See e.g. *Berrehab v Netherlands* (A/138) (1989) 11 EHRR 322.

The concept of 'family life' should also influence the interpretation of Art 10(2) of Regulation 1612/68 on freedom of movement for workers within the Community. Art 10(1) provides that (a) the worker's spouse and their descendants who are under 21 years old or are dependants and (b) dependent relatives in the ascending line 'shall, irrespective of their nationality, have the right to install themselves with a worker who is a national of one Member State and who is employed in the territory of another Member State'. Under Art 10(2), 'Member States shall facilitate the admission of any member of the family not coming within the provisions of paragraph 1 if dependent on the worker or living under his roof in the country whence he comes'. According to Strasbourg case law, 'family life' is not confined to families based on marriage; it may encompass other de facto relationships.[22] When deciding whether a relationship constitutes 'family life', relevant factors include whether the couple live together, the length of their relationship and whether they have demonstrated their commitment to each other by having children or by any other means.[23] Thus, 'any member of the family' should include unmarried and even same sex partners.[24]

Art 3 of Protocol No 4 articulates the principle that a State cannot expel its own nationals[25] or deny them entry to its territory.[26] Notwithstanding the EC Treaty's prohibition of discrimination on grounds of nationality,[27] therefore, the special duty owed by EU Member States to their own nationals means that the nationals of other Member States do not enjoy equal rights in all respects.[28]

3. Equality

Art 14 ECHR provides that the rights and freedoms set forth in the Convention shall be enjoyed by all persons without discrimination on any ground. In other words, Art 14 imposes an additional

---

[22] See e.g. X, Y and Z v United Kingdom (1997) 24 EHRR 143, para 36.
[23] Ibid.
[24] Especially in the light of Art 14 of the Convention. See below.
[25] See Case C-370/90 R v Immigration Appeal Tribunal and Surinder Singh, ex parte Secretary of State for the Home Department [1992] ECR I-4265, para 22.
[26] See Joined Cases C-65 and C-111/95 R v Secretary of State for the Home Department, ex parte Shingara [1997] All ER (EC) 577.
[27] Art 6 TEC (renumbered Art 12).
[28] For example, with regard to remedies in the event of exclusion on grounds of public policy. See Shingara, loc cit, at p 606, paras 28–30.

obligation on States to ensure equality in fields which are governed by the Convention. Discrimination occurs if 'the distinction has no objective and reasonable justification'.[29] While the margin of appreciation which States enjoy is sometimes broad, Strasbourg case law shows that discrimination on the grounds of sex is particularly serious and that very weighty reasons must be shown in justification.[30]

According to the ECJ, freedom from discrimination on the ground of sex is a fundamental human right the observance of which it has a duty to ensure.[31] The Court favours a broad interpretation of the right. In *P v S and Cornwall County Council*,[32] it ruled that, in the absence of justification, the dismissal of a transexual for a reason related to gender reassignment violated the Equal Treatment Directive.[33] It held that such discrimination was based, essentially if not exclusively, on the sex of the person concerned since 'he or she is treated unfavourably by comparison with persons of the sex to which he or she was deemed to belong before undergoing gender reassignment'.[34] Referring to the case of *Rees*,[35] where the Strasbourg Court observed that post-operative transsexuals form a 'fairly well-defined and identifiable group',[36] the ECJ stated that '[t]o tolerate such discrimination would be tanatamount, as regards such a person, to a failure to respect the dignity and freedom to which he or she is entitled and which the Court has a duty to safeguard'.[37] For his part, Advocate General Tesauro advocated 'a rigorous application of the principle of equality so that . . . any connotations relating to sex and/or sexual identity cannot be in any way relevant.'[38] He expressed the profound conviction that a universal value was at stake, namely the irrelevance of a person's sex with regard to the rules regulating relations in society.[39]

---

29 *Belgian Linguistic Case (No 2) (A/6)* (1968) I EHRR 252, para 10.
30 See e.g. *Abdulaziz, Cabales and Balkandali v United Kingdom (A/94)* (1985) 7 EHRR 471.
31 See e.g. Case 149/77, *Defrenne v Sabena (No 3)* [1978] ECR 1365.
32 Case C-13/94 [1996] ECR I-2143.
33 76/207/EEC
34 [1996] ECR I-2143, para 21.
35 *Rees v United Kingdom (A/106)* (1987) 9 EHRR 56.
36 Ibid, para 38.
37 [1996] ECR I-2143, para 22.
38 Ibid, at p 2154, para 19.
39 Ibid, p 2157, para 24.

There are similarities between the issues raised by discrimination against transsexuals and those raised by discrimination against homosexuals. Under the European Convention the status of homosexuals is even stronger than that of transsexuals. In *Dudgeon*,[40] for example, the Strasbourg Court described sexual life as 'a most intimate aspect' of private life covered by Art 8. And in May 1996, in a case concerning the homosexual age of consent in the United Kingdom, the European Commission of Human Rights declared admissible a complaint of a violation of Art 14 in conjunction with Art 8. Of persons aged over 16 but under 18, only homosexual males were prohibited from engaging in sexual conduct in accordance with their orientation. The applicant argued that between the ages of 16 and 18 he had the only sexual orientation under which he was precluded from any lawful possibility of expressing an important and intimate aspect of his personality.[41]

The question of whether Community law covers discrimination on the grounds of sexual orientation has been referred to the ECJ in two British cases. In *Grant v South-West Trains*,[42] the applicant's male predecessor was granted travel concessions for his common law wife, whereas the applicant was refused concessions for her same-sex partner. An industrial tribunal considered that the ECJ's decision in *P v S and Cornwall County Council* 'is at least persuasive authority for the proposition that discrimination on the ground of sexual orientation is unlawful'. It requested a preliminary ruling as to whether such discrimination is contrary to Art 119 of the EC Treaty or Art 2(1) of the Equal Treatment Directive. Bearing in mind that travel concessions for employees and members of their family constitute 'pay',[43] Advocate General Elmer concluded that there was gender discrimination contrary to Art 119 since the concessions were conditional on the cohabitee's being of the opposite sex to the employee; and that such discrimination could not be justified by reference to the fact that the employers's intention was to confer benefits on heterosexual couples as opposed to homosexual couples. The Advocate General observed that in *P v S and Cornwall County Council* the ECJ 'took a decisive step away from an interpretation of the principle of equal treatment based on the traditional comparison between a female

---

40 *Dudgeon v United Kingdom* (A45) (1982) 4 EHRR 149.
41 App No 25186/94 *Sutherland v United Kingdom* (1996) 22 EHRR CD 182.
42 Case C-249/96. (17 February 1998).
43 Case 12/81 *Garland* [1982] ECR 359

and a male employee'[44] and that conceptions of morality were ir-relevant to the Court's decision.[45] However, the ECJ held that there was no sex discrimination in *Grant* since South-West Trains also refused travel concessions to partners of gay men. It is hard to reconcile *Grant* with *P v S and Cornwall County Council*, where the Court rejected the United Kingdom's submission that no dis-crimination arose because the employer would also have dis-missed P if P had been a woman undergoing gender reassignment.

The *Grant* judgment would appear to determine the outcome of *R v Secretary of State for Defence, ex parte Perkins*,[46] which in-volves judicial review of the decision to discharge the applicant from the Royal Navy in pursuance of a policy to discharge anyone of homosexual orientation. Mr Perkins contends that the decision violated Art 2(1) of the Equal Treatment Directive. In an earlier case,[47] the Court of Appeal held that the Directive plainly did not extend to sexual orientation and refused to request a preliminary ruling on the question. Thorpe LJ stated: 'if the European Union is to proscribe discrimination on grounds of sexual orientation that must be achieved by a specific directive and not by an extended construction of the Directive of 1976.'[48]

Building upon its decision in *P v S and Cornwall County Coun-cil*, the ECJ could have ruled that discrimination on grounds of sexual orientation is contrary to the Equal Treatment Directive. As Lightman J observed in *Perkins*:

> there must be a real prospect that the European Court will take the further courageous step to extend protection to those of homosexual persuasion, if a courageous step is necessary to do so. I doubt however whether any courage is necessary, for all that may be required is working out and applying in a constructive manner the implications of the Advocate General's Opinion and the judgment in the *Cornwall* case.[49]

In *Grant*, however, the ECJ held that Community law does not

---

44 Para 15 of the Advocate General's opinion in Case C-249/96.
45 Ibid, para 17.
46 Case C-168/97 OJ 1997 No C 199/11.
47 *R v Secretary of State for Defence, ex parte Smith* [1996] QB 517.
48 Ibid, p 565.
49 [1997] IRLR 297 at 303(38).

cover discrimination based on sexual orientation.[50] With reference to Strasbourg case law from the 1980s and early 1990s, it concluded that stable homosexual relationships are not yet regarded as equivalent to marriages or stable relationships outside marriage between persons of opposite sex. Of course, since the Convention is a living instrument which should be construed in accordance with the values of today, decisions taken several years ago may not be a good guide to contemporary standards.

On the face of it, *Perkins* is a sexual orientation case covered by the ECJ's dictum in *Grant*. However, if it could be shown that the policy of dismissing homosexuals from the Royal Navy had a disparate adverse impact on men, there would be indirect sex discrimination.[51] In view of the protection accorded by the European Convention, this line of argument could not be dismissed lightly. If indirect discrimination were established, the Government would have to show 'very weighty reasons' by way of objective justification, bearing in mind that derogations from fundamental rights must be construed strictly and in accordance with the principle of proportionality.[52]

4. Freedom of information

The Strasbourg Court has repeatedly declared that pluralism, tolerance and broadmindedness are hallmarks of a democratic society which the Convention requires to be respected.[53] The right to freedom of information, which is enshrined in Art 10 ECHR, extends to information or ideas which offend, shock or disturb the State or any sector of the population.[54] It complements the right to privacy,[55] which is protected by the Community legal system[56] and

50 It should be noted that new Art 6a TEC (to be renumbered Art 13) will permit the Council to take appropriate action to eliminate various forms of discrimination, including discrimination based on sexual orientation. See further Chapter 7, section 3.2.1. In *Toonen v Australia* (1993) IHRR Vol 1 No 3 at p 105, para 87, the Human Rights Committee considered that the term 'sex' in the non-discrimination provision of the ICCPR (Art 26) included sexual orientation.

51 See e.g. J. Steiner and L. Woods, *Textbook on EC Law* (Blackstone Press, 5th ed, 1996), p 340.

52 Case 222/84 *Johnston v Chief Constable of the RUC* [1986] ECR 1651, paras 38 and 52.

53 See e.g. *Handyside v United Kingdom* (A/24) 1 EHRR 737, para 49.

54 Ibid.   55 Art 8 ECHR.

56 See e.g. Case 136/79 *National Panasonic v EC Commission* [1980] ECR 2033. See further section 4 below.

informs Community legislation.[57] The relevance of the freedom of information to the operation of the common market is illustrated by the ECJ's case law.

In *Grogan,*[58] the ECJ was asked to interpret Arts 59 and 60 EEC in the context of the prohibition by Irish law of the dissemination by an Irish students' association of information about the availability of abortion services in England. The defendants argued that the prohibition violated the freedom of expression and the freedom to receive and impart information enshrined in Art 10(1) of the Convention. The ECJ ruled that a medical operation, performed in accordance with the law of the State where it is carried out, constitutes a service within the meaning of Art 60.[59] However, it found no breach of Art 59, since the prohibition on the students did not restrict the activity of the clinics. There being no commercial link between the students' association and the clinics, the prohibition fell outside the scope of Community law and therefore Art 10 ECHR was not applicable.

The ECJ's judgment suggests that if the necessary commercial link had existed, it would have regarded the prohibition as falling within the scope of Community law, but would not have found a breach of Art 10. Advocate General Van Gerven opined that Art 10 applied because the national rule in question did not fall within the exclusive jurisdiction of the national legislature since it had 'effects in an area covered by Community law'.[60] Nevertheless, he concluded that the Irish authorities were entitled to take the view that the prohibition was acceptable in a democratic society.[61]

Just over a year later, however, in *Open Door Counselling and Dublin Well Woman v Ireland,*[62] the Court of Human Rights found a breach of Art 10 on the same facts. While acknowledging that 'the national authorities enjoy a wide margin of appreciation in matters of morals',[63] the Strasbourg Court was 'struck by the absolute nature of the Supreme Court injunction which imposed a "perpetual" restraint on the provision of information to pregnant women concerning abortion facilities abroad, regardless of age or state of health or their reasons for seeking counselling on the ter-

---

57 See e.g. Directive 95/46/EC of 24 October 1995 on the protection of individuals with regard to the processing of personal data and on the free movement of such data, O.J. 1995 No L 281/31.
58 Case C-159/90 [1991] ECR I-4685.
59 Ibid, para 21.   60 Ibid, p 4723, para 31.   61 Ibid, p 4729, para 38.
62 (A/246) (1993) 15 EHRR 244.   63 Ibid, para 63.

mination of pregnancy'.[64] On that ground alone the restriction appeared 'over broad and disproportionate',[65] an assessment which was confirmed by other factors.[66] The cases of *Grogan* and *Open Door Counselling* illustrate the potential for conflicting interpretations of the Convention by the two European Courts.

Freedom of expression issues commonly arise in relation to broadcasting. In *TV10 SA* v *Commissariaat Voor de Media*,[67] the ECJ was called upon to consider Arts 10 and 14 ECHR in the context of the Dutch authorities' refusal to allow TV10, a commercial broadcasting organisation established in Luxembourg but operated largely by Dutch nationals for a Dutch audience, access to the Dutch cable network. Finding that TV10 had established itself in Luxembourg in order to escape Dutch legislation (the *Mediawet*) applying to domestic broadcasting associations,[68] the Dutch authorities decided that TV10 could not be regarded as a foreign broadcaster; accordingly, its programmes could not be transmitted by cable in the Netherlands. The *Raad van State* asked the ECJ whether such restrictions were compatible with Community law, having regard to Arts 10 and 14 of the European Convention. The ECJ held that they were compatible. Regarding the Convention, it recognised that the *Mediawet* was designed to ensure a pluralist and non-commercial broadcasting system intended to safeguard the freedom of expression, 'which is precisely what the European Convention on Human Rights is designed to protect'.[69]

In the course of his Opinion, the Advocate General made an important observation concerning TV10's allegation of discrimination. The Dutch court had not asked the ECJ about the applicability of the Community law principle of non-discrimination, even though access to the Dutch cable network had in fact been granted to another Luxembourg broadcaster. The ECJ had been asked to consider the prohibition of discrimination only in connection with Art 14 ECHR. Advocate General Lenz noted that the Court's power of review was therefore more limited than if it had been invited to consider the prohibition of discrimination under Community law.[70] This was because Art 14 prohibits dis-

---

64 Ibid, para 73.   65 Ibid, para 74.
66 Ibid, paras 75–77.   67 Case C-23/93 [1994] ECR I-4795.
68 The case arose before the Television Broadcasting Directive (89/552/EEC) had to be transposed into national law and before the *Mediawet* was amended to allow commercial broadcasting.
69 Loc cit, note 67, paras 18, 25.   70 Ibid, p 4801, para 10.

crimination only with regard to the enjoyment of the rights and freedoms set forth in the Convention. It does not prohibit discrimination as such.

A corollary of the right to receive and impart information is the right of access to documents in the possession of the public authorities. In *The Netherlands v EU Council*,[71] where the Netherlands unsuccessfully argued that the Council had committed an abuse of power by basing rules on access to documents upon Art 151 TEC,[72] the ECJ recognised that 'the domestic legislation of most Member States now enshrines in a general manner the public's right of access to documents held by public authorities as a constitutional or legislative principle';[73] and that at Community level the importance of that right had been confirmed on various occasions, 'in particular in the declaration on the right of access to information annexed to the Final Act of the Treaty on European Union, which links that right with the democratic nature of the institutions'.[74] The Court did not specifically mention the ECHR or any other human rights treaty. However, Advocate General Tesauro referred to various Council of Europe documents[75] linking the right of access to documents in the possession of the public authorities and the right to freedom of expression and to receive and impart information, enshrined in Art 10 ECHR and Art 19 ICCPR. He concluded that 'the right of access to information is increasingly clearly a fundamental civil right'.[76]

5. Competition investigations and proceedings

Certain provisions of the European Convention are very important in the context of EC competition investigations and proceedings. Art 6 contains the Convention's fair trial guarantees, which must

---

71 Case C-58/94 [1996] ECR I-2169.
72 Which authorises the Council to adopt its Rules of Procedure.
73 Loc cit, note 71, para 34.
74 Declaration 17: 'The Conference considers that openness of the decision-making process strengthens the democratic nature of the institutions and the public's confidence in the administration.'
75 E.g. Recommendation 854 (1979) of the Parliamentary Assembly of 1 February 1979 and Recommendation R (81) 19 of the Committee of Ministers of 25 November 1981.
76 Loc cit, note 71, p 2180, para 16. The Amsterdam Treaty introduces a right of access to European Parliament, Council and Commission documents: see new Art 191a TEC (renumbered Art 255).

be respected in the determination of criminal charges or of civil rights and obligations. Art 6(1) provides, *inter alia*, that '[i]n the determination of his civil rights and obligations or of any criminal charge against him, everyone is entitled to a fair and public hearing within a reasonable time by an independent and impartial tribunal established by law'.

According to Strasbourg case law, one of the criteria for being a tribunal within the meaning of Art 6 is independence of the executive.[77] Since the executive power of the Community is largely vested in the Commission, the latter cannot constitute a tribunal.[78] Neither is it subject to Art 6(1) in respect of its investigative functions. This is because 'essentially investigative' functions do not attract the Convention's fair trial guarantees: 'a requirement that such a preparatory investigation should be subject to the guarantees of a judicial procedure as set forth in Art 6(1) would in practice unduly hamper the effective regulation in the public interest of complex financial and commercial activities'.[79]

Nevertheless, natural and legal persons are entitled to the protection of Art 6 when defending EC competition proceedings, since the Convention's fair trial guarantees must be secured to any person '[i]n the determination of his civil rights and obligations or of any criminal charge against him'. The case of *Société Stenuit* v *France*[80] suggests that EC competition proceedings are 'criminal' in nature.[81] There, the Strasbourg Commission unanimously held that a French company fined for anti-competitive behaviour had faced a 'criminal charge' within the meaning of Art 6.[82] The Commission was influenced by the fact that under French law, fines of up to five per cent of their annual turnover could be imposed on companies as a deterrent. According to Regulation 17/62, fines of up to ten per cent of annual turnover can be imposed by the EC Commission for breaches of EC competition rules. Alternatively, EC competition proceedings involve the determination of 'civil rights and obligations', which includes all proceedings the result of which

---

77 See e.g. *Ringeisen* v *Austria No 1)* (A/13) 1 EHRR 455, para 95.
78 See e.g. Joined Cases 100–103/80 *Musique Diffusion Française* v *Commission* [1983] ECR 1825, para 7. The ECJ followed its earlier decision in Joined Cases 209–215 and 218/78 *Van Landewyck* v *Commission* [1980] ECR 3125.
79 *Saunders* v *United Kingdom* (1997) 23 EHRR 313, para 67.
80 (A/232-A) (1992) 14 EHRR 509.
81 See P Duffy, 'The human rights dimension to competition practice', Lawyers' Europe, Summer 1994, p 6.
82 The case was subsequently struck out by the Court.

is decisive for private rights and obligations,[83] especially actions which are pecuniary in nature.[84] Civil rights and obligations will be in issue when competition proceedings do not result in the imposition of fines but nevertheless have serious consequences for the companies concerned.[85]

In *Orkem* v *Commission*,[86] the ECJ held that the EC Commission could not compel an undertaking to answer questions which might involve an admission by the undertaking concerned of the existence of an infringement. However, Regulation 17/62 could be used 'to compel an undertaking to provide all information concerning such facts as may be known to it and to disclose to [the Commission], if necessary, such documents relating thereto as are in its possession, even if the latter may be used to establish, against it or another undertaking, the existence of anti-competitive conduct'.[87] The ECJ's approach may be compared with that of the Court of Human Rights. In *Funke* v *France*,[88] the Strasbourg Court held that anyone charged with a criminal offence has the right to remain silent and not to contribute to incriminating himself.[89] Similarly, in *Saunders* v *United Kingdom*[90] it found a violation of Art 6(1) where statements compulsorily given by the applicant to DTI inspectors during a fraud investigation were subsequently used by the prosecution at his criminal trial. The Court held that the right to silence and the right not to incriminate oneself, though not specifically mentioned in Art 6, are generally recognised international standards which lie at the heart of the notion of a fair procedure.[91] Moreover, it rejected the government's submission that only statements which are directly incriminating fall within the privilege against self-incrimination.[92] In *Murray* v *United Kingdom*,[93] however, the Strasbourg Court made it clear that the aim of Art 6 is to provide protection against 'improper compulsion' by the authorities. Without deciding what constitutes 'improper compulsion', it held that the right to silence is not absolute and that, in the circumstances of that case, the drawing of ad-

83 *König* v *Germany* (A/27) 2 EHRR 170, para 90.
84 *Editions Periscope* v *France* (A/234-B) (1992) 14 EHRR 597, para 40.
85 Duffy, op cit.
86 Case 374/87 [1989] ECR 3283.
87 Ibid, para 34.
88 (A/256-A) (1993) 16 EHRR 297.
89 Ibid, para 44.
90 Loc cit, note 79.   91 Ibid, para 68.
92 Ibid, para 71.   93 (1996) 22 EHRR 29.

verse inferences from the accused's silence did not infringe Art 6. It distinguished *Funke* in terms of the degree of compulsion involved.[94] The role of the EC Commission in competition proceedings is compatible with the Convention provided that undertakings subsequently have the right to due process on all aspects of the case before a judicial body having full jurisdiction and fulfilling the standards of independence and impartiality required by Art 6.[95] Judicial control by the CFI and the ECJ fulfil the Convention's requirements only if all the issues are fully considered and no discretionary reserve is shown in relation to Commission findings of fact and/or economic evidence. Appeals to the CFI must be equated with a first-instance criminal trial involving a thorough examination of all the evidence and respect for the presumption of innocence and rights of the defence.[96]

There is also the question of delay. Competition investigations by the EC Commission and subsequent appeals to the CFI and thereafter to the ECJ can take several years. Under Art 6(1) of the Convention, however, there is a right to a determination by a court 'within a reasonable time'. What constitutes a reasonable time must be decided in the light of the circumstances of each case.[97] In particular, it involves an analysis of the complexity of the case and of the conduct of the applicant and the relevant authorities. On the latter point, the importance of what is at stake for the applicant must be taken into account.[98] The 'reasonable time' requirement is very important in competition cases, particularly when Commission proceedings cause parallel national proceedings to be stayed.[99]

Also relevant to competition investigations is Art 8 ECHR, which guarantees the right to respect for private and family life,

---

94 Ibid, paras 44–49. The Convention's 'fair hearing' requirements are not necessarily the same in civil cases as in criminal proceedings. See *Dombo Beheer BV v Netherlands* (A/274-A) (1994) 18 EHRR 213.

95 See e.g. *Fischer v Austria* (A/312) (1995) 20 EHRR 349. 'Full jurisdiction' includes the power to quash, on questions of fact and law, the decision of the body below. See *Palaoro v Austria* (A/329-B), para 43.

96 Duffy, op cit.

97 It is worth noting that Strasbourg proceedings invariably involve lengthy delays, though this should change when Protocol No 11 enters into force. See Chapter 2, section 3.4.

98 See e.g. *Allenet de Ribemont v France* (A/308) (1995) 20 EHRR 557, para 47; *Vernillo v France* (A/198) (1991) 13 EHRR 880, para 30.

99 See Case C-234/89 *Delimitis v Henninger Bräu* [1991] ECR I-935.

home and correspondence. In *Hoechst v Commission*,[100] noting that there was no Strasbourg case law on the subject, the ECJ held that the protective scope of Art 8 did not extend to business premises.[101] A power of search without prior judicial authorisation was considered to be implicit in Art 14 of Regulation 17/62. In *Niemietz v Germany*,[102] however, the Strasbourg Court held that Art 8 extended to professional or business premises and had been infringed by the search of a lawyer's office. Similarly, in *Halford v United Kingdom*[103] it held that telephone calls made from business premises may be covered by the notions of 'private life' and 'correspondence.' Accordingly, there must be no interference with the exercise of the rights enshrined in Art 8(1) 'except such as is in accordance with the law and is necessary in a democratic society in the interests of national security, public safety or the economic well-being of the country, for the prevention of disorder or crime, for the protection of health or morals, or for the protection of the rights and freedoms of others'.[104]

6. The right to property

Within the European Convention system, the right to property is guaranteed by Art 1 of Protocol No 1:

> Every natural or legal person is entitled to the peaceful enjoyment of his possessions. No one shall be deprived of his possessions except in the public interest and subject to the conditions provided for by law and by the general principles of international law.

> The preceding provisions shall not, however, in any way impair the right of a State to enforce such laws as it deems necessary to control the use of property in accordance with the general interest or to secure the payment of taxes or other contributions or penalties.

Art 1 comprises three distinct rules. The first, which is expressed in the first sentence of the first paragraph and is of a general nature,

---

100 Joined Cases 46/87 and 277/88 [1989] ECR 2859.
101 Ibid, para 18. Cf. Case 136/79 *National Panasonic v Commission* [1980] ECR 2033.
102 (A/251-B) (1993) 16 EHRR 97.
103 (1997) 24 EHRR 523.
104 Art 8(2) ECHR.

lays down the principle of peaceful enjoyment of property. The second rule, in the second sentence of the same paragraph, covers deprivation of possessions and subjects it to certain conditions. The third, contained in the second paragraph, recognises that Contracting States are entitled, *inter alia*, to control the use of property in accordance with the general interest. The second and third rules, which are concerned with particular instances of interference with the right to peaceful enjoyment of property, must be construed in the light of the general principle laid down in the first rule.[105]

Interference with the right to property is permitted only in the public interest. The notion of 'public interest' is extensive and the domestic legislature enjoys a wide margin of appreciation in implementing social and economic policies. The Strasbourg Court will respect the latter's judgment as to what is 'in the public interest' unless that judgment is manifestly unreasonable.[106] Moreover, any interference must strike a fair balance between the demands of general interest and the requirements of the protection of the individual right to property. In particular, there must be a reasonable relationship of proportionality between the means employed and the aim sought to be achieved by any measure depriving a person of his possessions.[107]

In *Stran Greek Refineries*,[108] the Strasbourg Court held that a final and binding arbitration award was a 'possession' within the meaning of Art 1 of Protocol No 1 since it conferred upon the applicants a right in the sums awarded. Legislative annulment of the award violated the Convention because it upset the balance between the protection of the right to property and the requirements of public interest. That judgment could be important in the context of Community law, given that Member States can be liable in damages for their breaches of Community law.[109] It should cer-

---

105 See e.g. *Holy Monasteries v Greece* (A/301-A) (1995) 20 EHRR 1.
106 *Pressos Compania Naviera SA v Belgium* (A/332) (1996) 21 EHRR 301, para 37.
107 *Stran Greek Refineries and Stratis Andreadis v Greece* (A/301-B) (1995) 19 EHRR 293.
108 Ibid.
109 See e.g. Joined Cases C-6 and 9/90 *Francovich v Italian Republic* [1991] ECR I-5357; Joined Cases C-46 and 48/93 *Brasserie du Pêcheur v Federal Republic of Germany* and *R v Secretary of State for Transport, ex parte Factortame Ltd* [1996] ECR I-1029; Joined Cases C-178, 179 and 188-90/94 *Dillenkofer v Federal Republic of Germany* [1996] ECR I-4845.

tainly be noted by any Member State which may be tempted to refuse to pay damages which are awarded against it.[110]

Bearing in mind the importance of intellectual property rights in Community law, it is appropriate to consider whether a patent application constitutes a 'possession' within the protective scope of Art 1. In *British-American Tobacco Co Ltd v Netherlands*,[111] following a Dutch decision that the subject-matter of a patent application lodged by BAT was not patentable, the Strasbourg Commission held that there had been no interference with the applicant's right to property since Art 1 of Protocol No 1 applies only to existing possessions and does not guarantee the right to acquire property.[112] The Commission's conclusion was consistent with previous Strasbourg case law.[113] Although BAT were denied a protected intellectual property right, they were not deprived of their existing property.

The right to property was acknowledged as a principle of Community law in *Hauer*.[114] Although it is often invoked in the context of the Common Agricultural Policy, it is very difficult to establish a violation. This is because the ECJ considers that the right to property is subject to restrictions justified by objectives of general interest pursued by the Community, provided that the restrictions do not constitute a disproportionate and intolerable interference with the very substance of the right.[115] Thus, it has been held that the right to property is not violated by the reduction of milk quotas without compensation.[116] Furthermore, it does not include the right to dispose for profit of an advantage, such as reference quantities allocated in the context of the common organisation of a market, which does not derive either from the assets or from the occupational activity of the person concerned. Accordingly, the ECJ has held that the right to property does not require a Member

---

110 Disregard for Community law can lead to Strasbourg proceedings Cf. *Hornsby v Greece* (1997) 24 EHRR 250, where the Strasbourg Court found a violation of Art 6(1) ECHR following Greece's failure to comply with the ECJ's judgment in Case 147/86 *Commission v Greece* [1988] ECR 1637.
111 (A/331-A) (1996) 21 EHRR 409.
112 Ibid, para 71 of the Commission's Report. The Court found it unnecessary to decide the issue.
113 See *Van der Mussele v Belgium* (A/70) (1984) 6 EHRR 163, para 48; App No 11628/85, *Linde v Sweden*, DR 47, p 270.
114 Case 44/79 *Hauer v Land Rheinland-Pfaltz* [1979] ECR 3727. See Chapter 3.
115 See e.g. Case C-280/93 *Germany v EU Council* [1994] ECR I-4973.
116 See e.g. Joined Cases T-466, 473, 474 and 477/93 *O'Dwyer v EU Council* [1995] ECR II-2071.

State to introduce a scheme for payment of compensation by a landlord to an outgoing tenant in respect of reference quantities originally awarded to the latter and transferred to the former on the expiry of a lease; nor does it confer a right to compensation directly on the tenant.[117]

7. Environmental protection

Under Art 173(4) of the EC Treaty, individuals who seek the annulment of Community acts which are not addressed to them must, establish 'direct and individual concern'.[118] Despite relaxation of the *locus standi* requirements,[119] they remain too stringent, particularly where the interests affected by the act in question are not economic but environmental. The case of *Greenpeace International* v *Commission*[120] illustrates this well. Sixteen private individuals and three environmental associations sought the annulment of a Commission decision granting Spain financial assistance from the European Regional Development Fund for the construction of two power stations in the Canary Islands. The Court of First Instance declared the application inadmissible. Observing that 'persons other than the addressees of a decision may claim that it is of direct and individual concern to them only if it affects them by reason of certain attributes which are peculiar to them, or by reason of factual circumstances which differentiate them from all other persons and thereby distinguish them individually in the same way as the person addressed', the Court held that the private applicants were not individually concerned; they were affected by the decision in the same manner as any other local resident, fisherman, farmer or tourist. The Court rejected the argument that it should free itself from the constraints imposed by previous case law and concentrate solely on the fact that the applicants had suffered or would suffer detriment or loss from the harmful environmental effects of unlawful conduct by the Community.

---

117 Case C-2/92 *R* v *MAFF, ex parte Bostock* [1994] ECR I-955. See also Case C-38/94 *R* v *MAFF, ex parte Country Landowners Association* [1995] ECR I-3875.

118 See e.g. Steiner and Woods, op cit, Ch 28.

119 See e.g. Case C-309/89 *Codorniu* v *Council* [1994] ECR I-1853; Case T-482/93 *Weber* v *Commission* [1996] ECR II-609.

120 Case T-585/93 [1995] ECR II-2205.

As for *Greenpeace* and the other associations, the Court found that they had not adduced any special circumstances to demonstrate the individual interest of their members. The possible effect of the contested decision on the legal position of their members was no different from that alleged by the private applicants. The Court rejected the pleas that an exchange of correspondence and a meeting between Greenpeace and the Commission constituted special circumstances such as to give it *locus standi*. Those exchanges were for purposes of information only, since the Commission was under no duty either to consult or to hear the applicants.

The CFI was unmoved by the fact that, in the practice of national courts in matters relating to environmental proteciton, *locus standi* may depend merely on showing a sufficient interest.[121] The applicants have appealed to the ECJ.[122] There is a compelling argument that the standing requirements of Art 173(4) should be interpreted more liberally, not only in accordance with the principle of effective judicial protection[123] and in the light of the obligation to integrate environmental and health protection requirements into Community policies and activities,[124] but also in conformity with Strasbourg standards.[125] The European Convention guarantees the right of access to a court in civil matters[126] and the right to an effective remedy[127] in respect of arguable complaints of breaches of its provisions. Environmental misconduct can be a violation of the Convention, even though the latter does not enshrine the right to environmental protection as such. In *Lopez Ostra v Spain*,[128] the Court of Human Rights found a violation of Art 8 of the Convention[129] on account of nuisance caused by a waste treatment plant. It observed that 'severe environmental pollution may affect indi-

---

[121] See e.g. *R v HM Inspectorate of Pollution and MAFF, ex parte Greenpeace Ltd* [1994] 2 CMLR 548.

[122] Case C-321/95P. At a sitting of the full Court on 23 September 1997, Advocate General Cosmas proposed that the appeal be dismissed in its entirety.

[123] See Chapter 4.

[124] See Arts 129(1) and 130r(1) TEC. The integration principle has been strengthened by the Amsterdam Treaty.

[125] Particularly as, by virtue of the Amsterdam Treaty, the ECJ has jurisdiction over Art F(2) TEU (which states that the Union shall respect fundamental rights as guaranteed, *inter alia*, by the European Convention on Human Rights) 'with regard to action of the institutions'. See Chapter 7.

[126] Art 6(1).

[127] Art 13.

[128] (A/303-C) (1995) 20 EHRR 277.

[129] Art 8 protects the right to respect for private and family life, home and correspondence.

viduals' well-being and prevent them from enjoying their homes in such a way as to affect their private and family life adversely'.[130] The respondent State had not struck a fair balance between the interest of the town's economic well-being (that of having a waste-treatment plant) and the applicant's enjoyment of her right to respect for her home and her private and family life.

This outline of the interface between EU law and the European Convention on Human Rights illustrates how important it is for EU lawyers to be familiar with the Convention and Strasbourg case law. Just as no British lawyer can afford to be ignorant of Community law, so no EU lawyer can afford to ignore the Convention which, despite being the product of a separate international organisation, has special significance in and for the European Union. Within the framework of Community law, the Convention constrains the institutions and the Member States, and it has a vital part to play in the interpretation and application of EU provisions.

---

130 (1995) 20 EHRR 277 at 295, para 51.
131 See Chapter 2.

CHAPTER SIX

Opinion 2/94 and the protection of human rights in the EU

1. Introduction

In April 1994, pursuant to Art 228(6) TEC, the Council asked the Court of Justice for an Opinion on the following question: 'Would the accession of the European Community to the Convention on Human Rights and Fundamental Freedoms of 4 November 1950 be compatible with the Treaty establishing the European Community?'[1]

The Council's request for an Opinion marked a key stage in a process which had started in 1979, when the accession of the European Community to the Convention was first formally proposed by the Commission.[2] The ECJ had indicated its willingness to help resolve the technical and legal problems surrounding accession, and on 30 November 1993, meeting for the first time under the EU's Third Pillar,[3] the Justice Council decided to consult the Court on the legal questions arising from adherence to the Convention.[4] The purpose of Art 228(6) is to forestall complications which would result from legal disputes concerning the compatibility with the Treaty of international agreements binding on the Community.[5] The request for an Opinion raised two main legal issues: the legal basis of accession to the Convention[6] and the compatibility of accession with the EC Treaty.[7] However, it was not

---

1 OJ 1994 No C 174/8. Under Art 228(6), if the ECJ's opinion is adverse the agreement in question may enter into force only in accordance with Art N TEU.
2 See Chapter 3.
3 Title VI TEU (CJHA)
4 See EUROPE No 6118, 1 December 1993, p 7. It is surprising that this decision was made in the context of an intergovernmental pillar of the EU.
5 Opinion 3/94 [1995] ECR I-4577, para 16.
6 The Community must observe the limits of the competences conferred upon it by the Treaties.
7 Especially since Arts 164 and 219 TEC confer exclusive jurisdiction upon the Court of Justice in actions between the Community and its Member States.

for the ECJ to consider the Community's treaty-making capacity in public international law or to determine whether the European Convention itself created any obstacles to accession. Nor could the Court express a view on the desirability of accession.[8]

The Council stated its own position on the scope of accession, Community participation in the Convention's control bodies and the modifications which would have to be made to the Convention and its Protocols. Written and oral observations were submitted by the Commission, the European Parliament and most of the Member States. There was a measure of agreement. For example, that an Amending Protocol to the Convention (rather than an Optional Protocol) would have to be concluded in order to facilitate Community accession; that it would be the European Community which acceded to the Convention, since the EU lacked legal personality and therefore treaty-making capacity; and that each Community could adhere to the Convention only within the framework of its own powers. Beyond that, however, there was no consensus. The Community institutions and the governments of Austria, Belgium, Denmark, Finland, Germany, Greece, Italy and Sweden considered that, in the absence of specific enabling provisions, Art 235 TEC would serve as the legal basis for accession; and that accession, in particular the submission of the Community to the legal system of the Convention, would not be contrary to Arts 164 and 219 of the Treaty. In contrast, the French, Spanish and Portuguese governments, Ireland and the United Kingdom argued against any application of Art 235 and denied that accession would be compatible with the Treaty.[9]

2. Opinion 2/94: The ECJ's response to the Council

Having heard the Advocates General,[10] the ECJ delivered its Opinion on 28 March 1996.[11] It concluded that, while the request for

---

8 *Report of the Court of Justice on Certain Aspects of the Application of the Treaty on European Union*, Proceedings of the Court of Justice and the Court of First Instance, No 15/95, para 19.

9 The respective submissions are outlined in the Report for the Hearing.

10 See Art 108(2) of the Court's Rules of Procedure.

11 Opinion 2/94 *Accession by the Community to the Convention for the Protection of Human Rights and Fundamental Freedoms* [1996] ECR I-1759.

an Opinion was admissible,[12] it could not give an opinion on the compatibility with the Treaty of Community accession to the Convention, since it had insufficient 'information regarding the arrangements by which the Community envisages submitting to the present and future judicial control machinery established by the Convention'.[13] It also ruled that, 'as Community law now stands, the Community has no competence to accede to the Convention'.[14] In particular, Art 235 could not be used as a legal basis:

> That provision, being an integral part of an institutional system based on the principle of conferred powers, cannot serve as a basis for widening the scope of Community powers beyond the general framework created by the provisions of the Treaty . . . . On any view, Article 235 cannot be used as a basis for the adoption of provisions whose effect would, in substance, be to amend the Treaty without following the procedure which it provides for that purpose.[15]

While acknowledging that respect for human rights is a condition of the lawfulness of Community acts,[16] the Court ruled that accession to the Convention would entail a substantial modification of the Community system for the protection of human rights, a modification of such constitutional significance that it could be brought about only by way of Treaty amendment.[17]

3. The implications of Opinion 2/94 for human rights in the EU

As far as the protection of human rights in the EU is concerned, the most important aspect of the Opinion is the ECJ's declaration that respect for human rights is a condition of the lawfulness of Community acts. This constitutes a clear and unambiguous statement of the current legal position which had long been implicit in the Court's case law. Against that background, it may be observed

---

12 Ibid, para 18. Ireland and the United Kingdom, as well as the Danish and Swedish governments, had argued that the request was premature since an agreement was not yet envisaged.
13 Ibid, para 20.
14 Ibid, para 36.
15 Ibid, para 30.
16 Ibid, para 34.
17 Ibid, paras 34–35.

that the Court's conclusion about Art 235 represents not a lack of concern for human rights but proper concern that the Community should act strictly within the limits of its existing powers. Nevertheless, the conclusion itself is open to question since the protection of human rights underlies all Community action.[18] This was essentially the position taken by the Council, the Commission, the Parliament and the majority of the Member States. If the effective realisation of the Community's objectives requires accession to the Convention and supervision by the Strasbourg Court, Art 235 would seem to offer a sufficient legal basis. Moreover:

> The Member States are all bound by the Convention and subject to the jurisdiction of the Strasbourg Court. They cannot escape their Convention obligations, nor the Strasbourg supervision, by transferring sovereign powers to the European Communities. In that situation it is not self-evident, to say the least, that these Member States cannot unanimously, through the Council and on the basis of Article 235, make the exercise of Community powers subject to those same obligations and that same jurisdiction as far as the protection of human rights is concerned.[19]

By ruling as it did, the ECJ avoided some of the more difficult issues raised by the Council's request for an Opinion. In particular, it remains unclear whether accession to the Convention would jeopardise the autonomy of the Community's legal order. Opponents of accession consider that it would be unacceptable for decisions of the ECJ to be subject to review by another body. In principle, however, this would not present a problem. In *Opinion 1/91*,[20] the ECJ accepted the Community's submission to a court created by international agreement for the interpretation and application of that agreement, provided that the autonomy of the Community legal order was not affected. There is no reason to believe that accession to the Convention would undermine the autonomy of the Community legal order.[21] While legally binding, the

---

18 P van Dijk, *Judicial Protection of Human Rights in the European Union – Divergence, Co-ordination, Integration*, University of Exeter, Centre for European Legal Studies, Exeter Paper in European Law, No 1 (1996), pp 8–9.

19 Ibid, p 8.

20 Opinion 1/91 *Re the Draft Treaty on a European Economic Area* [1991] ECR I-6079.

21 Cf. the original version of the EEA agreement, according to which the EEA Court would have determined the interpretation not only of the agreement but also of the corresponding rules of Community law.

judgments of the Court of Human Rights could not directly repeal or amend provisions of Community law. Moreover, the Convention already forms part of the EU's constitutional order[22] and the Court of Justice generally defers to Strasbourg case law in order to interpret and apply the rights and freedoms enshrined within it.[23] This is entirely appropriate, since the Court of Human Rights is the authoritative interpreter of the Convention and Europe's principal judicial organ for the protection of human rights. In these circumstances, accession would essentially formalise the status of the Convention in the Community legal order and institutionalise the deference (self-limitation) already shown by the ECJ.

Nevertheless, it would be appropriate to amend Art 164 TEC, which provides that '[t]he Court of Justice shall ensure that in the interpretation and application of this Treaty the law is observed'.[24] A second paragraph should be added to that article in order to acknowledge the authority of the Court of Human Rights with regard to the interpretation and application of the Convention. To the extent that the Court of Justice is part of the 'single institutional framework' which serves the EU,[25] this would be a corollary of Art F(2) TEU which requires 'the Union' to respect fundamental rights as guaranteed by the Convention.

4. The legal and institutional implications of Community accession to the Convention

By acceding to the Convention, the Community would submit to the machinery for individual and inter-State applications. However, actions between the Community and its Member States would have to be excluded in recognition of the monopoly conferred in such matters upon the Court of Justice by Art 219 TEC. Would the Community, not being a State, have any difficulty in fulfilling its Convention obligations? After all, the Convention contains many concepts which presuppose statehood, including 'national security', 'territorial integrity' and 'economic well-being of the country'.[26] Nevertheless, the need to restrict certain rights

---

22 Art F(2) TEU (renumbered Art 6(2)).
23 See Chapter 4.
24 Renumbered Art 220 TEC.
25 See Arts C and E TEU (renumbered Arts 3 and 5, respectively).
26 See e.g. Arts 8–11 ECHR.

on the grounds of an overriding interest applies to the Community no less than to sovereign States. The Accession Protocol could thus provide that the Convention, when it uses terms which relate to States, applies *mutatis mutandis* to the Community.[27] In order to avoid difficulties arising from the uneven application of the Convention and its Protocols among the EU Member States, accession would have to be confined to the Convention and any Protocols which had come into force and been ratified by all the Member States.[28] Moreover, it would not have any effect on the reservations entered by the Member States, which would continue to apply in the areas falling outside the scope of Community law.

According to the House of Lords Select Committee on the European Communities, the main obstacles to Community accession to the Convention are institutional.[29]

4.1 Community participation in Strasbourg control bodies

Other Convention parties might object to the Community's 'double representation' both through its Member States and through the Community as such,[30] and be concerned that EU Member States could thereby block decisions which called into question Community acts. Particularly sensitive has been the issue of representation on the Committee of Ministers, a political body with quasi-judicial functions[31] whose members are bound by instructions from national governments. However, the Committee of Ministers will lose its decision-making role when Protocol No 11 enters into force.[32] As for the Court of Human Rights, it is desirable that there should be Community participation in the form of

---

27 *Accession of the Communities to the European Convention for the Protection of Human Rights and Fundamental Freedoms*, EC Bulletin, Supp 2/79, para 20 (hereafter 'Commission Memorandum').

28 Currently only Protocol No 1 (protection of property, right to education, right to free elections).

29 House of Lords Select Committee on the European Communities, *Human Rights Re-examined* (Session 1992–93, 3rd Report, HL Paper 10), paras 95–96 (hereafter 'HLSC Report').

30 L Neville Brown and Tom Kennedy, *The Court of Justice of the European Communities* (Sweet & Maxwell, 4th edn, 1994), p 370.

31 In the absence of a referral to the Court of Human Rights, the Committee of Ministers currently decides whether there has been a violation of the Convention. See Chapter 2, section 3.3.3.

32 But it will continue to supervise the execution of the Strasbourg Court's judgments. See Chapter 2, section 3.4.

a judge who would not be a member of the ECJ at the same time.[33] Moreover, since Strasbourg judges act purely in a personal capacity and *not* as national representatives, Community participation need not be restricted to cases involving complaints against the Community. There should be a Community contribution to the development of all Convention case law, not only because the latter impacts upon Community law, but also, and more importantly, because it helps to shape the constitutional order of Europe.

4.2 Delay

Since a Strasbourg application can be entertained only after domestic remedies have been exhausted,[34] a more serious obstacle to Community accession is the prospect of long delays caused by cumulating litigation. Within the framework of the Convention, decisions of the ECJ would be regarded as decisions of a national court.[35] On average, ECJ proceedings take about 18 months in the case of references for preliminary rulings, nearly 21 months in the case of direct actions, and over 21 months in respect of appeals from the CFI. Direct actions before the latter take 23 months.[36] The Strasbourg procedure is generally even slower. On average it takes five years for a case to be resolved under the Convention.[37] While direct recourse to Strasbourg might be possible in some cases following Community accession,[38] others would involve 'successively having to climb ladders to Luxembourg and to Strasbourg'.[39] As the Select Committee suggested, the incidence of delay could be reduced by allowing the ECJ to refer questions about the interpretation of the Convention to the Strasbourg Court.

---

[33] Besides the fact that a dual mandate would be undesirable, under Protocol No 11 the Strasbourg Court will be a permanent body.

[34] Art 26 ECHR. See Chapter 2, Section 2.3.1.

[35] Commission Memorandum, para 24.

[36] L Neville Brown, 'The first five years of the Court of First Instance and appeals to the Court of Justice: Assessment and statistics' (1995) 32 CMLRev 743, 749.

[37] In *D* v *United Kingdom* (1997) 24 EHRR 423, however, the Court gave judgment less than 15 months after the applicant, who was dying of AIDS, lodged his application with the Commission.

[38] For example, where a person claiming a violation of his human rights by the Community had no *locus standi* under Art 173 TEC.

[39] House of Lords Select Committee Report, loc cit, note 29, para 99. However, this does not necessarily deter litigants. See e.g. Case C-159/90 *SPUC* v *Grogan* [1991] ECR I-4685 and *Open Door Counselling and Dublin Well Woman* v *Ireland* (A/246) (1993) 15 EHRR 244.

National courts could similarly be permitted to request preliminary rulings from the latter in the context of domestic challenges to Community acts.[40] That would require an amendment to the Convention, however.

5. Is Community accession to the Convention necessary?

In the light of *Opinion 2/94*, the most urgent question is whether the EC Treaty should be amended to permit the accession of the Community to the Convention.[41] Arnull takes the view that accession is unnecessary:

> The House of Lords Select Committee on the European Communities has examined the question of accession on two occasions, once in 1980[42] and again in 1992.[43] On both occasions the Committee opposed accession on the basis that any benefits would be marginal and that the Community had more pressing tasks. That seems to me to be even more true today.[44]

Nevertheless, accession would arguably have important legal and political advantages. In particular, it would protect individuals should the Convention be disregarded by Community institutions. There will be a gap[45] in the protection of human rights as long as Community acts and ECJ decisions cannot be reviewed in Strasbourg,[46] however rare instances of conflict between the ECJ and

---

40 See the Opinion of Advocate General Warner in Case 130/75 *Prais v Council* [1976] ECR 1589 at 1607.

41 A M Arnull, *Opinion 2/94 and its Implications for the Future Constitution of the Union*, in *The Human Rights Opinion of the ECJ and Its Constitutional Implications*, University of Cambridge, CELS Occasional Paper No 1, June 1996, p 7.

42 House of Lords Select Committee on the European Communities, *Human Rights* (Session 1979–80, 1st Report, HL 362).

43 See note 29.

44 Arnull, op cit, p 8. Cf. the Opinion of the Economic and Social Committee of the European Communities on 'The European Union and the external dimension of human rights policy', April 1997, 3.1.2 (CES 474/97) (hereafter 'ECOSOC Opinion').

45 Commission Communication on Community Accession to the ECHR and to certain of its Protocols, EC Bull 10/90, 1.3.218 (hereafter 'Commission Communication').

46 See e.g. *CFDT v European Communities* [1979] 2 CMLR 229. See further Resolution 1068 (1995) of the Parliamentary Assembly of the Council of Europe, (1995) 38 YECHR, vol 2, p 965.

the Court of Human Rights may be.[47] Indeed, Community accession to the Convention would be consistent with the development of a legal order which is no longer directed at economic operators but at citizens of the Union.[48] As the Commission has argued, 'the European citizen has a legitimate interest in having his rights *vis-à-vis* the Community laid down in advance'.[49] To the disadvantage of States, as well as of individuals, legal certainty is also compromised by the fact that two European Courts independently resolve human rights issues with reference to the same Convention.[50]

Accession would also be of symbolic importance,[51] particularly because it would strengthen the democratic legitimacy of the EU's institutional framework and procedures.[52] Besides improving the image of Europe as an area of freedom and democracy, accession would have political advantages beyond the EU.[53] It would symbolise the common values which make up European citizenship and identity, and enhance the credibility of action taken by the Community and the Member States to defend human rights in the world. In particular, it would consolidate respect for human rights in those countries of Central and Eastern Europe which have become members of the Council of Europe and are preparing to join the EU.[54] Due respect for human rights is now emphasised in the context of admission to membership of the European Union.[55] In practice, it is a requirement that candidate States should be parties to the European Convention and accept the right of individual petition and the jurisdiction of the Strasbourg Court.[56] In other words, respect for human rights is a foundation for the construc-

---

47 See the Opinion of Advocate General Jacobs in Case C-168/91 *Konstantinidis* [1993] ECR ECR I-1191, paras 50–51.
48 This point was made by the European Parliament in its observations to the ECJ. See *Opinion 2/94*, Report for the Hearing.
49 Commission Memorandum, para 5.
50 Siofra O'Leary, '*Accession by the European Community to the European Convention on Human Rights – The Opinion of the ECJ*' [1996] EHRLR 362 at 365.
51 Ibid, p 369.
52 Cf. Case C-300/89 *Commission* v *Council* [1991] ECR I-2869, para 20.
53 Commission Memorandum, para 14.
54 C Duparc, *The European Community and Human Rights* (Commission of the European Communities, Oct 1992), p 19.
55 See the first sentence of Art O TEU as supplemented by the Amsterdam Treaty (renumbered Art 49). See further Chapter 7, section 3.2.
56 Both of which will be compulsory under Protocol No 11 to the Convention. See Chapter 2, section 3.4.

tion of Europe.[57] It is also a key element of the Community's relations with third countries.[58] According to Art 130u(2) TEC, for example, Community policy in the area of development cooperation 'shall contribute to the general objective of developing and consolidating democracy and the rule of law, and to that of respecting human rights and fundamental freedoms'. In these circumstances, the Community's failure to accede to the ECHR and to submit its own conduct to Strasbourg review is, at best, anomalous.[59]

But is the European Convention the most appropriate human rights instrument for the Community in the late 1990s and beyond? What about socio-economic, environmental and minority rights? Would it not be better for the Community to create a catalogue of human rights specifically adapted to its own requirements? Since the Convention is concerned more with civil and political rights and freedoms than with economic and social rights,[60] it might be considered to be of marginal interest to the Community. However, the classic rights and freedoms are not unimportant in the Community context.[61] In any case, accession to the Convention need not preclude the preparation of a Community Bill of Rights.[62] It could be the first step towards the elaboration of a Bill of Rights incorporating not only civil and political rights but also economic, social and cultural rights, as laid down in the European Social Charter.[63]

[57] See the European Parliament's 'Resolution on human rights', OJ 1991 No C 240/45; and the ECOSOC Opinion, loc cit, note 44.

[58] See D McGoldrick, *International Relations Law of the European Union* (Longman, 1997).

[59] Brown and Kennedy, op cit, p 369.

[60] The distinction is sometimes more apparent than real. See e.g. *Lopez Ostra v Spain* (A/303-C) (1995) 20 EHRR 277 and *Sigurjonsson v Iceland* (A/264) (1993) 16 EHRR 462. See further Chapter 1, section 1.1.

[61] See Chapter 5.

[62] See Commission Communication and Duparc, op cit, p 19. Cf HLSC Report, loc cit, note 29, para 79.

[63] See ECOSOC Opinion, section 3.1.3 and the Declaration of Fundamental Rights and Freedoms adopted by the European Parliament on 12 April 1989, OJ 1989 No C 120/151.

6. Community accession to the European Social Charter

In view of the importance of socio-economic rights in the Community context, it is no less appropriate for the Community to consider acceding to the (revised) European Social Charter. Indeed, it has been suggested that the Charter is a better source of binding standards for the Community than the Convention.[64] In his evidence to the House of Lords Select Committee on the European Communities,[65] Professor Hepple observed that in terms of its content, the Charter is closer to the Treaty of Rome, the Community Charter of Fundamental Social Rights for Workers and the Maastricht Agreement on Social Policy.

Not surprisingly, there are sharp differences of view as to the desirability and feasibility of Community accession to the ESC. For some scholars, the ECJ's conclusions in *Opinion 2/94* regarding accession to the Convention apply *a fortiori* since accession to the Charter would imply an expansion of the Community's powers in the area of social rights.[66] However, others conclude that Community accession to the Charter is both necessary and possible. They argue that the objections expressed in *Opinion 2/94* were based on the particular institutional implications of the Convention's supervisory system and observe that the supervisory mechanisms of the Convention and the Charter are 'widely divergent'.[67]

In the light of *Opinion 2/94*, it is at least arguable that Art 235 TEC could be the basis of Community accession to the (revised) European Social Charter.[68] The ECJ did not deny that respect for human rights is a Community objective for the purposes of Art 235; it merely excluded recourse to Art 235 as a legal basis for fundamental constitutional and institutional changes.[69] While the Charter clearly constitutes 'a distinct international institutional

---

64 O'Leary, op cit, p 370.
65 *Human Rights Re-examined*, Session 1993–1994, 18th Report, p 19.
66 A W Heringa, *Social Rights and the Rule of Law*, Council of Europe Colloquy on The Social Charter of the 21st Century, Strasbourg, May 1997, p 17 (Doc SCColl/rep9e).
67 International Federation of Human Rights Leagues, *Observations on the revised European Social Charter,* Council of Europe Colloquy on the Social Charter in the 21st Century, Strasbourg, May 1997, p 9 (Doc SCColl/rep8e). See further Chapter 2.
68 See Chapter 2, section 4.3.
69 Arnull, op cit, p 7. Cf. A A Dashwood, *Commentary,* ibid, pp 26–7.

system',[70] it can be argued that accession to it would not 'entail a substantial change in the Community system for the protection of human rights'.[71]

All 15 EU Member States are parties to the original European Social Charter, 'the signing and ratification (of which) gave expression to a common political will and entailed recognition of common values'.[72] Although the ESC's scope is wider than that of the Community Charter of Fundamental Social Rights for Workers, there is a degree of overlap.[73] To the extent that the Turin Charter deals with matters which are covered by Community law, the EU Member States already apply its provisions in accordance with their Community obligations.[74] Of course, in so far as the Charter concerns matters which are outside the scope of Community law, there is no such constraint upon them.[75]

Hepple observes that the European Social Charter provides a basis for social action within a far wider geographical area than the present Community, and that it is important for the Community to be seen to be supporting this wider 'social constitution of Europe'. A separate Community Charter, he warns, is damaging to European integration because it builds a social wall around the Community.[76] As the Parliamentary Assembly of the Council of Europe has declared,[77] 'it is important to preserve the concept of a European social space covering all the countries of the Council of Europe, including those of the European Community, EFTA, and which may be extended to the countries of Central and Eastern Europe which are likely to accede in increasing numbers to the Council of Europe'.

Community accession to the Convention and the (revised) European Social Charter would arguably strengthen the EU's human rights policy, based as it is on the principles of universal and indivisible human rights and the interdependence between human

70 *Opinion 2/94*, loc cit, para 34.
71 Ibid.
72 Case 236/87 *Bergemann* v *Bundesanstalt für Arbeit* [1988] ECR 5125 at 5137 (*per* Advocate General Lenz).
73 See Chapter 3, section 7.1.
74 See e.g. the Commission's Communication concerning the signing by Community Member States of the [first] Additional Protocol to the European Social Charter, COM(88) 218 final.
75 Cf. Case C-337/91 *Van Gemert-Derks* v *Bestuur Van De Nieuwe Industriele Bedrijfsvereniging* [1993] ECR I-5435.
76 Hepple, op cit, para 12(4).
77 Resolution 831/1989.

rights, democracy and development.[78] Community accession would certainly boost the Charter's significance as a European Bill of Social Rights. As things stand, however, quite apart from any legal obstacles, it is unlikely that the necessary consensus will be found among the Member States, especially as none of them has yet ratified the revised Charter.

---

[78] ECOSOC Opinion, section 3.2.1.

CHAPTER SEVEN

The future of human rights protection in the European Union

1. Introduction

In the previous chapters we have examined various developments with regard to the protection of human rights in the European Union. One of the most notable aspects is that, despite several attempts, there has not yet been agreement among the Member States to complete the Community legal order with a written catalogue of rights which are protected within the Community framework. Discussions on the adoption of a Bill of Rights have led nowhere. Accession to the European Convention of Human Rights is also blocked by political resistance.

From a legal point of view, it is difficult to see why human rights protection should cause such a problem for the Community. While their 'constitutional traditions' may not be as common as the ECJ would have us believe, the Member States all subscribe to the principles of the rule of law, democracy and respect for human rights. They have made that clear to the international community by signing and ratifying a number of international human rights instruments. The most important of these is the European Convention on Human Rights. All 15 Member States have ratified the Convention (though not all of the Optional Protocols) and are bound by its provisions, yet to date attempts to incorporate them formally into the Community legal order have failed. It is true that Art F(2) TEU refers to the Convention, but only as a matter of principle. Furthermore, it appears that the constitutional court of at least one Member State is prepared to challenge the most fundamental principles of Community law because of the Community's unwillingness to include express human rights provisions

INTRODUCTION

in its law. The guarantees provided by the ECJ's case law and political declarations of goodwill are considered insufficient.[1]

This being so, why has it been so difficult to complete the Community legal order with a written catalogue of human rights which are protected within the context of Community law? Some lawyers tend to seek the answer in the differences of legal effect between traditional human rights treaties and Community law. Others observe that the European Convention is not directly enforceable in all domestic legal orders,[2] fearing that such effect may be gained through the backdoor via Community law. They point to the ECJ's sometimes 'liberal' case law, which may result in a domino effect, especially as 'the framework of Community law' is not clearly defined.[3] Even though, on accession, the European Convention would become Community law and not national law, there could, as now, be legal repercussions within the Member States. As we have seen:

> breaches of the Convention's norms can be argued within the context of challenges to the validity of Community acts which are at the root of the domestic measure that is purportedly violating a human rights provision therein; or, alternatively, the domestic court can be persuaded to request an interpretation of the relevant Community act under Article 177 in the light of its compatibility with the provisions enumerated in the European Convention.[4]

Added to this, the ECJ influences national law through its development of far-reaching principles of Community law. Examples can be found in recent cases where the Court required national procedures or remedies to be invented or ignored in order to give guarantees which national law did not provide.[5]

In short, the twin concerns about ECJ activism and the domestic implications of Community accession to the ECHR are very real. There is much resistance in some Member States to any extension of the jurisdiction of the ECJ and of the Court of Human Rights. Moreover, even the ECJ itself may be reluctant to submit to Stras-

---

1 See Chapter 3, section 5.
2 Notably the United Kingdom. See section 4 below, however.
3 See Chapter 4.
4 Andrew Drzemczewski, *European Human Rights Convention in Domestic Law* (Oxford, 1983), p 259.
5 See e.g. Case 271/91 *Marshall v Southampton and South West Hampshire Area Health Authority (No 2)* [1993] ECR I-4367 and Case C-213/89 *R v Secretary of State for Transport, ex parte Factortame Ltd (No 1)* [1990] ECR I-2433.

bourg scrutiny, which would be required if the Convention became part of Community law.

Nevertheless, the continued failure to create a Bill of Rights for the Community could threaten the continuation of the Community legal order as such, as demonstrated by the *Banana* cases.[6] This issue should therefore be resolved as a matter of urgency. In the run-up to the revision of the Maastricht Treaty, many groups lobbied hard to draw it to the Member States' attention. In this chapter we discuss the results. First, we look at the report of the *Comité des Sages*, then we analyse the relevant provisions of the Amsterdam Treaty. Finally, we consider the implications for the EU of the proposed incorporation of the European Convention into United Kingdom law.

2. A Europe of civic and social rights?

On the basis of its 1995 Social Action Programme, the Commission established a committee (the *Comité des Sages*) to examine the future of the Community Charter of Fundamental Social Rights of Workers in connection with the review of the Treaties. The Committee met for the first time in October 1995. In March 1996 it published its Report, the contents of which addressed a much wider problem than the future of the Community Charter.

The title of the Report is not without significance. Instead of using the wider term 'civil' rights, the Committee opted for 'civic' rights. The latter is hardly ever used in international law. The difference between the two terms is that the former refers to the basic rights of every person within a certain jurisdiction, whereas the latter is connected with the status of 'citizen'. Few textbooks on the international protection of human rights refer to 'civic' rights.[7]

This suggests that as far the *Comité des Sages* is concerned, any Community catalogue of rights should be addressed to the citizens of the European Union, rather than to everyone within the territory of the Member States. This reflects the lack of political support for the extension of rights to third-country nationals. The wording of new Art 6a of the EC Treaty confirms this: although it

---

6 See Chapter 3, section 5.
7 See, however, K A Betterman, F L Neuman and H C Nipperdey, *Die Grundrechte* (Berlin, 1996), vol I/1, p 10.

is very broad, it omits the prohibition of discrimination on grounds of nationality.[8]

On the basis of two hypotheses, the Committee formulated a number of general objectives for the 1996 IGC to take into account in the process of revising the Treaties. It was assumed that social issues now lie at the heart of the challenges facing the European Union; and that the current structure of civic and social rights and social policies in Europe is extremely complex. This led to general recommendations to:

- specify immediately a minimum core of fundamental rights as a first stage;
- set in motion a participatory process to formulate an up-to-date list of civic and social rights and duties; and
- integrate social policies into the Union's normal operations.

One of the most notable features of the Report is that the Committee, while emphasising the importance of social rights, proceeds on the basis of the interdependence of social and civic rights, which, 'in the European tradition, are inseparable'.[9] Within this framework, 'citizenship' is presented as a major element in the equation. Consequently, the conclusion is that the Treaty should incorporate 'certain fundamental social and civic rights and should reflect the Union's determination to formulate a Bill of Rights to guide us at the dawn of the 21st century'.[10]

No fewer than 26 proposals were tabled, which are not always very clear. Some address problems of social and employment policies. Others address fundamental rights issues. The latter include the following:

- nurture the emergence of a new generation of civic and social rights, reflecting technological change, enhanced awareness of the environment and demographic change;[11]
- strengthen the sense of citizenship and democracy in the Union by treating civic and social rights as indivisible;[12]

---

8 See section 3.2.1. below.
9 Maria de Lourdes Pintasilgo, who chaired the Committee, in her foreword.
10 Ibid.
11 Proposal IV.
12 Proposal V.

■ enshrine in the Treaties a basic set of fundamental civic and social rights (in the form of a Bill of Rights), specifying which rights should have immediate force of law and which should be dealt with in more detail at a second stage. All these rights would be available to the citizens of the European Union, while some of them might also be available to third-country nationals, provided that the conditions were right.[13] At the second stage, a full list of civic and social rights and duties should be compiled;[14]

■ include among these rights a ban on any form of discrimination on the basis of race, colour, sex, language, religion, political or other opinion, national or social origin, membership of a national minority, wealth, birth, disability or any other situation;[15]

■ by way of exception, postulate the principle that each Member State must establish, subject to its own conditions, a minimum income for persons who cannot find paid work and have no other sources of income;[16]

■ give the ECJ jurisdiction over Art F TEU;[17]

■ rather than acceding to the ECHR, introduce special arrangements for legal remedy in respect of the violation of fundamental rights, in the form of a specific appeal court made up of non-permanent judges from the Member States' constitutional or supreme courts.[18]

3. Human rights provisions in the TEU

The draft Treaty of Amsterdam suggests that little attention has been paid to the recommendations of the *Comité des Sages*. Its provisions reveal nothing of a comprehensive approach to human rights protection in the EU, nor is there any sign of a Bill of Rights in the making. A number of the Comittee's recommendations have been followed, but that may have been due to a wider political movement. For example, the non-discrimination provision[19] was

13 Proposal VII.
14 Proposal XIII.
15 Proposal VIII.
16 Proposal IX.
17 Proposal XI.
18 Proposal XII.
19 See section 3.2.1 below.

long overdue. Similarly, the new Title on Employment was largely the result of political pressure before and during the Amsterdam Conference in June 1997. Before examining the main new provisions, we recall the human rights provisions contained in the Maastricht Treaty.

3.1 Human rights provisions in the 1992 Maastricht Treaty

The third recital of the Maastricht Treaty's preamble confirms the commitment of the Member States 'to the principles of liberty, democracy and respect for human rights and fundamental freedoms and the rule of law'. Article F(1) TEU provides that the Union 'shall respect the national identities of its Member States, whose systems of government are founded on the principles of democracy'. Article F(2) provides that:

> The Union shall respect fundamental rights, as guaranteed by the European Convention for the Protection of Human Rights and Fundamental Freedoms ... and as they result from the constitutional traditions common to the Member States, as general principles of Community law.

Article F(3) added that the Union 'shall provide itself with the means necessary to attain its objectives and carry through its policies'. Although there is no explicit reference to human rights in that provision, we may assume that the objectives and policies mentioned here relate to the protection of human rights.

The Treaty's provisions on a common foreign and security policy include Art J.1(2), which states that the policy's objectives shall be, *inter alia*, 'to develop and consolidate democracy and the rule of law, and respect for human rights and fundamental freedoms'.

With regard to CJHA, Art K.2(1) provides that the matters of common interest referred to in Art K.1 (designed to achieve the objectives of the Union, in particular the freemovement of persons) shall be dealt with in compliance with the European Convention on Human Rights 'and the Convention relating to the Status of Refugees of 28 July 1951[20] and having regard to the protection afforded by Member States to persons persecuted on political grounds'. The reference to the free movement of persons in Art K.1 is not a reference to the free movement of workers as pro-

[20] For text, see I Brownlie, *Basic Documents on Human Rights* (Oxford, 3rd edn, 1992), p 64.

tected by Arts 48 *et seq.* of the EC Treaty. The measures mentioned in Art. K.1 relate, *inter alia*, to asylum policy, immigration policy and policy regarding third-country nationals and police cooperation for the purposes of preventing international crime. The value of Arts F, J and K of the Maastricht Treaty was greatly diminished by Art L. By virtue of that article the ECJ has no jurisdiction over the TEU, except for those provisions which amend the foundation Treaties, the third sub-paragraph of Art K.3(2)(c) (which states that international conventions drawn up by the Council in the areas referred to in Art K.1 may provide for the ECJ to interpret their provisions and rule on disputes regarding their application) and Arts L to S (final provisions). The implications of this for the protection of human rights in the EU have been noted with concern by the Court itself.[21] On the other hand, Art L does not detract from the Court's human rights case law, which forms part of the *acquis communautaire*, or deny the justiciability of human rights in Community law.[22]

3.2 Human rights provisions in the 1997 Treaty of Amsterdam[23]

The first thing to note is that a new fourth recital has been added to the TEU's preamble. It reads: 'Confirming their attachment to fundamental social rights as defined in the European Social Charter . . . and the 1989 Community Charter of the Fundamental Social Rights of Workers.' This interesting amendment is reinforced by a similar reference to both Charters in new Art 117 TEC.[24] In Chapter 2 we observed that the preamble to the Single European Act recognised the European Social Charter as an instrument to be respected within the Community legal order. For some obscure reason, however, there was no reference to the Single European Act in the Maastricht Treaty. Although there can be little doubt as to where the Union's priorities lie, it is a hopeful sign that the ESC

---

21 See Chapter 3, section 4.1.
22 See S O'Leary, *Aspects of the Relationship between Community Law and National Law* in *The European Union and Human Rights*, N A Neuwahl and A Rosas (eds) (Martinus Nijhoff, 1995), p 45.
23 The Treaty was signed on 2 October 1997. Below we refer to the articles of the TEU and TEC as amended, both in their original form and as subsequently renumbered.
24 Renumbered Art 136 TEC.

has reappeared. On the other hand, it is still not mentioned along-side the Convention in Art F.[25] This is further evidence that the Member States value social rights less highly than civil rights.

In terms of the protection of human rights, the most significant developments concern judicial control and enforcement, reflecting the Member States' desire to establish an area of freedom, security and justice.[26] First, a large part of the original TEU's third pillar (Title VI, CJHA) has been brought within the EC Treaty[27] and becomes subject to interpretation and review by the ECJ. This helps to address concern about the lack of judicial protection for individuals with regard to such matters as asylum and immigration. However, the Court will not have jurisdiction to rule on any measure or decision taken with a view to ensuring the absence of internal border controls if it relates to the maintenance of law and order and the safeguarding of internal security.[28] There is a parallel exclusion of jurisdiction with regard to similar aspects of the *Schengen acquis* relating to the abolition of checks at common borders,[29] which is brought within the institutional and legal framework of the EU and is otherwise subject to judicial control.[30]

Secondly, Art L[31] TEU has been amended to give the Court jurisdiction over Art F(2)[32] 'with regard to action of the institutions, insofar as [it] has jurisdiction under the Treaties establishing the European Communities and under this Treaty'. Accordingly, the ECJ now has jurisdiction to ensure that in the interpretation and application of Art F(2) the law is observed by the institutions. However, there is no amendment of Art F(2) itself. Accordingly, the basis of the ECJ's jurisdiction regarding the protection of human rights is unchanged. In other words, the Court must continue to found its human rights protection on general principles of law rather than on the European Convention as such. The

25 Renumbered Art 6 TEU.
26 See e.g. Art B (fouth indent), renumbered Art 2 TEU.
27 See Title IV of the EC Treaty: 'Visas, asylum, immigration and other policies related to free movement of persons' (Arts 61–69 TEC).
28 See Art 73p, renumbered Art 68 TEC.
29 The *Schengen acquis* is defined in the annex to the Schengen Protocol. It refers, in particular, to the Schengen Agreement of 14 June 1985 and the Schengen Convention of 19 June 1990. At present, Ireland and the United Kingdom are not bound by the *acquis* or, with Denmark, by new Title IV.
30 See Art 2 of the Protocol integrating the *Schengen acquis* into the framework of the European Union.
31 Renumbered Art 46 TEU.
32 Renumbered Art 6(2) TEU.

unfortunate message continues to be that the Member States are willing to treat the Convention as part of the EU's constitutional order, but only as a statement of principle.

Thirdly, the exclusion of the Court's jurisdiction over Title VI has been lifted, at least in part. New Art K.1[33] provides that, without prejudice to the powers of the European Community:

> the Union's objective shall be to provide citizens with a high level of safety within an area of freedom, security and justice by developing common action among the Member States in the fields of police and judicial cooperation in criminal matters and by combating racism and xenophobia.

The kind of 'common action' envisaged is set out in new Arts K.2 and K.3.[34] It covers such matters as operational cooperation in relation to the prevention, detection and investigation of crime and extradition between Member States. By virtue of Art L, as amended, the ECJ is given jurisdiction over Title VI under the conditions provided for by new Arts K.7[35] and K.12.[36] According to the former, the Court will be able to give preliminary rulings on the validity and interpretation of Council decisions, on the interpretation of Conventions and on the validity and interpretation of implementing measures at the request of national courts (provided that the Member State concerned has declared that it accepts such jurisdiction). It will also have jurisdiction to review the legality of Council decisions and to rule on any dispute between Member States regarding the interpretation or application of acts adopted under Art K.6(2)[37] whenever such dispute cannot be resolved by the Council itself. However, the Court will not be able to review the validity or proportionality of operations carried out by national police forces or the exercise of the responsibilities incumbent upon Member States with regard to the maintenance of law and order and the protection of internal security.[38]

The ECJ's newly conferred jurisdiction over Title VI of the TEU will therefore be limited. Moreover, a non-binding Declaration appended to the Final Act provides that 'Action in the field of

---

[33] Renumbered Art 29 TEU.
[34] Renumbered Arts 30 and 31 TEU, respectively.
[35] Renumbered Art 35 TEU.
[36] Renumbered Art 40 TEU, this regulates the establishment of closer cooperation between two or more Member States.
[37] Renumbered Art 34(2) TEU.
[38] New Art K.7(5), renumbered Art 35(5) TEU.

police cooperation under Art K.2, including activities of Europol,[39] shall be subject to appropriate judicial review by the competent national authorities in accordance with rules applicable in each Member State'. The European Parliament has expressed concern at the democratic deficit caused not only by the fact that negotiations and agreements in this field remain entirely in the hands of governments, but also because it remains unclear which court, if any, can exercise judicial control.[40]

As far as Art F[41] is concerned, most of the amendments seem to involve rewording, although some of the new words are significant. In particular, Art F(1) now provides that 'The Union is founded on the principles of liberty, democracy, respect for human rights and fundamental freedoms, and the rule of law, principles which are common to the Member States'. This specifies and makes more explicit the principles on which the legal orders of the Member States are based. It is a political statement more or less repeating the Statute of the Council of Europe, by which all (present and prospective) EU Member States are bound. As mentioned above, the emphasis is on civil and political rights, although implicitly there is recognition of social rights as they form part of the constitutions of most of the Member States.

The most important difference is the introduction of a procedure for enforcing the principles on which the Union is founded. New Art F.1[42] reads:

1. The Council, meeting in the composition of the Heads of State or Government and acting by unanimity on a proposal by one third of the Member States or by the Commission and after obtaining the assent of the European Parliament, may determine the existence of a serious and persistent breach by a Member State of principles mentioned in Article F(1), after inviting the government of the Member State concerned to submit its observations.

2. Where such a determination has been made, the Council, acting by a qualified majority, may decide to suspend certain of the rights deriving from the application of this Treaty to the Member State in question, including the voting rights of the representative of the

---

[39] The European Police Office established by the Europol Convention based on Art K. 3 of the Maastricht Treaty. See OJ 1995 No C 316/1.
[40] EUROPE/Documents No 2044, 3 July 1997.
[41] Renumbered Art 6 TEU.
[42] Renumbered Art 7 TEU.

government of that Member State in the Council. In doing so, the Council shall take into account the possible consequences of such a suspension on the rights and obligations of natural and legal persons. The obligations of the Member State concerned under this Treaty shall in any case continue to be binding on that State.

3. The Council, acting by a qualified majority, may decide subsequently to vary or revoke measures taken under paragraph 2 in response to changes in the situation which led to their being imposed.

4. For the purposes of this Article, the Council shall act without taking into account the vote of the representative of the government of the Member State concerned. Abstentions by members present in person or represented shall not prevent the adoption of decisions referred to in paragraph 1. A qualified majority shall be defined as the same proportion of the weighted votes of the members of the Council concerned as laid down in Article 148(2)[43] of the Treaty establishing the European Community.

The provisions of this paragraph shall also apply in the event of voting rights being suspended pursuant to paragraph 2.

5. For the purposes of this Article, the European Parliament shall act by a two thirds majority of the votes cast, representing a majority of its members.

The first observation must be that, despite the potentially grave consequences of a determination that there is a serious and persistent breach by a Member State of principles on which the Union is founded, the ECJ has no role at all in the enforcement procedure. This is confirmed by Art L. Although the Court has been given jurisdiction over Art F(2) 'with regard to action of the institutions',[44] it has no jurisdiction with regard to human rights violations by Member States outside the framework of Community law. Such violations may be actionable in Strasbourg, however.

Art F.1 embodies a purely political procedure to be initiated by the Member States or the Commission. The European Parliament, although involved in the determination of a breach, has no right of initiative. The procedure itself is rather cumbersome. The first step is for one-third of the Member States (or the Commission) to pro-

43 Renumbered Art 205.
44 See above.

pose the determination of a 'serious and persistent' breach of principles mentioned in Art F(1). This is likely to lead to considerable debate, since there must not only be a breach, but a serious and persistent breach. Assuming that the European Parliament's assent is obtained, there must then be unanimity within the Council on all three issues ('breach', 'serious' and 'persistent'). Once those hurdles have been overcome, a qualified majority of the Council must be prepared to suspend certain rights of the State involved. This is an extremely serious matter, so agreement will not easily be reached. On the other hand, if a matter is considered serious enough the Member States have demonstrated that they are able and willing to take drastic measures with regard to one of their number. We need only recall the action of the Community in relation to the United Kingdom over BSE.

As mentioned above, the new Art F.1 procedure should be distinguished from the judicial procedures which operate in the event of human rights violations in the application of Community law by the institutions or the Member States. The ECJ's jurisdiction in such cases is not affected by Art F.1. Within the framework of Community law, a Member State may be required to pay damages to an aggrieved individual, but the Court cannot suspend the State's membership rights.

The new procedure does not relate directly to the application of Community law as such. It creates the possibility of suspending a Member State which, in a purely domestic context, violates the basic principles referred to in Art F(1), which include respect for human rights and fundamental freedoms. The procedure would apply, for instance, if a Member State were guilty of gross and systematic violations of the human rights of its own citizens or third-country nationals, or if it were to replace a constitutional order based on democratic principles with a dictatorship. Although this may seem unlikely, we should not forget that some of the Member States only quite recently emerged from dictatorship and that many prospective Member States have limited experience of democratic principles.

It seems clear that Art F.1 prevails over Art F(3), which provides that 'The Union shall respect the national identities of its Member States'. Indeed, in view of Art F(3) *juncto* Art F.1, the Union shall not respect the national identity of a Member State if that identity changes from a democratic constitutional order based upon the rule of law into a dictatorship of any kind.

The new provisions in Art F.1 have led to parallel amendments of the foundation Treaties. Thus, new Art 236(1) TEC[45] provides that where a Member State's voting rights have been suspended in accordance with Art F.1(2) TEU, they shall also be suspended with regard to the EC Treaty. Similarly, where the existence of a serious and persistent breach has been determined in accordance with Art F.1(1), the Council may decide to suspend certain of the rights deriving from the application of the EC Treaty to the State concerned. Such decisions are presumably subject to review by the ECJ, unlike those taken in pursuance of Art F.1 itself.

Art F.1 is also referred to in a new Protocol to the EC Treaty on asylum for nationals of EU Member States. The Protocol provides that, given the level of protection of fundamental rights and freedoms by the Member States, Member States shall be regarded as constituting safe countries of origin in relation to asylum matters. Accordingly, any application for asylum made by a national of a Member State may be considered or declared admissible by another Member State only in certain cases. For example, if the Art F.1 procedure has been initiated in respect of the State of which the applicant is a national; or if the Council has determined the existence of a serious and persistent breach by that State of principles mentioned in Art F.1; or if the State in question has invoked Art 15 ECHR in order to derogate from its obligations under the Convention.[46]

With these new provisions, the Amsterdam Treaty seems to have adopted the essence of the Statute of the Council of Europe, which is very much concerned with respect for democratic principles and the rule of law, including the protection of human rights. This is interesting in view of the difficulty that Member States have in clearly and unequivocally adopting the European Convention on Human Rights as an integral part of Community law. However, it is less strange than at first sight. It is one thing to counteract threats to democracy as such; it is another to accept that, in the application of Community law, the ECJ should be able to review each and every failure of a Member State to respect fully the human rights of its citizens.

Despite the ECJ's human rights case law, Member States remain reluctant to provide the Court with a stronger and more explicit

45 Renumbered Art 309 TEC.
46 See further Chapter 2, section 2.1.

basis for the protection of human rights. In Chapter 3 we pointed out that such reluctance may be self-defeating. Once again, Germany's Constitutional Court may have to shock the EU's institutions and political leaders into realising this.

3.2.1 A new anti-discrimination provision

From the outset, the Treaty of Rome has prohibited discrimination on the grounds of nationality and sex.[47] Whereas the latter pursues a double aim which is both economic and social,[48] however, the former has nothing to do with human rights. It is merely intended to ensure the proper functioning of the Common Market. Moreover, the free movement of persons essentially applies only to EU citizens. In terms of human rights protection, therefore, the Treaty itself discriminates against third-country nationals.

This situation has not been changed by the inclusion of a general non-discrimination provision. New Art 6a TEC[49] provides:

> Without prejudice to the other provisions of this Treaty and within the limits of the powers conferred by it upon the Community, the Council, acting unanimously on a proposal from the Commission and after consulting the European Parliament, may take appropriate action to combat discrimination based on sex, racial or ethnic origin, religion or belief, age or sexual orientation.

In addition, appended to the Final Act is a non-binding Declaration which states that the institutions of the Community shall take account of the needs of persons with a disability.

There are some striking features about the new provision. First of all, it is not a directly effective provision upon which individuals can rely. It creates the possibility for the Commission to submit proposals to combat discrimination on certain grounds. Such proposals do not necessarily have to aim for 'hard' law. The Commission can adopt the 'soft' law approach of non-binding guidelines, codes of conduct, recommendations, etc. The effect of such instruments is unclear. For instance, the effect of the Code of Practice on measures to combat sexual harassment[50] has never been properly examined.

---

47 Arts 6 and 119 TEC, renumbered Arts 12 and 141.
48 Case 43/75 *Defrenne* v *Sabena* (No 2) [1976] ECR 455.
49 Renumbered Art 13 TEC.
50 OJ 1992 No L 49/1.

If the Commission were to opt for a 'hard law approach', it would probably meet with much more resistance from Member States in the Council. This is reflected in the wording of the provision, which states that the Council 'may take appropriate action'. Another feature is that the new article covers various grounds of discrimination. Since there is no reference to nationality,[51] however, the position of third-country nationals remains unaltered. It is perhaps surprising that 'sexual orientation' survived all drafts. By providing a basis for action by the Community to eliminate discrimination based on sexual orientation, the new provision offers the possibility of initiatives to complement Art 119 and the Equal Treatment Directive, which deal only with sex discrimination.[52] In short, it helps to promote human dignity and the principle of equality before the law.

3.2.2 A declaration on the abolition of the death penalty

Appended to the Amsterdam Final Act is a Declaration on the abolition of the death penalty:

> With reference to Art F(2) of the Treaty on European Union, the Conference recalls that Protocol No 6 to the [European Convention on Human Rights], and which has been signed and ratified by a large majority of Member States, provides for the abolition of the death penalty.

> In this context, the Conference notes that since the signature of the above-mentioned Protocol on 28 April 1983, the death penalty has been abolished in most of the Member States of the Union and has not been applied in any of them.

Italy wanted the abolition of the death penalty added to the principles recognised in Art F(1) TEU but the other Member States disagreed. The above non-binding Declaration represents a political compromise which seems to send a clear message to countries which aspire to EU membership. However, in view of the specific reference to Art F in Art O as amended,[53] the first sentence of which provides that 'Any European State which respects the principles set out in Art F(1) may apply to become a member of the

---

51 Cf. Art 14 ECHR.
52 See Chapter 5, section 3.
53 Renumbered Art 49 TEU.

Union', it appears that prospective Member States are not required to accept abolition. Nevertheless, the Declaration reflects the fact that the Union's human rights policy is informed by the law and practice of the Member States. It is their behaviour which ultimately determines the credibility of human rights protection in the EU. With this in mind, we turn to the proposed incorporation of the European Convention into UK law.

4. The incorporation of the ECHR into UK law

As a matter of public international law, the 15 EU Member States are all bound by the European Convention on Human Rights and by the rulings of the Strasbourg Court. Moreover, all except the United Kingdom and the Republic of Ireland have incorporated the Convention into domestic law, and Ireland's Bill of Rights largely reflects the substance of the Convention. Only in the United Kingdom are individuals unable to enforce their Convention rights directly in national courts, therefore.[54] While the Convention influences UK proceedings by resolving legislative ambiguity, guiding the exercise of judicial discretion and influencing the common law,[55] people within UK jurisdiction who seek the Convention's protection must lodge petitions in Strasbourg under Art 25 having exhausted their domestic remedies.[56]

The situation is made worse by the fact that to litigate in Strasbourg usually involves considerable cost and delay. While other countries which have incorporated the Convention into domestic law have had as many cases brought against them in the Court of Human Rights, it is the serious nature of the cases brought and the absence of speedy and effective domestic remedies which distinguishes the United Kingdom's record.[57] Besides the obvious disadvantages for individuals, the fact that the Convention is not part of UK law means that British judges are less able to influence the development of Convention jurisprudence. More specifically, they

[54] See e.g. *R v Morrissey* and *R v Staines* [1997] TLR 231.
[55] See e.g. *AG v Guardian Newspapers Ltd* [1987] 1 WLR 1248, *AG v Guardian Newspapers Ltd (No 2)* [1990] 1 AC 109, and *R v Secretary of State for the Environment, ex parte NALGO* (1993) 5 Admin LR 785.
[56] See Chapter 2.
[57] Jack Straw MP and Paul Boateng MP, 'Bringing Rights Home: Labour's Plans to Incorporate the European Convention on Human Rights into UK Law' [1997] EHRLR 71 at 74.

are unable to build up a body of case law on the Convention which is sensitive to British legal and constitutional traditions.[58]

This undesirable situation is about to change. The new British government is committed to incorporating the European Convention into UK law,[59] a move which is strongly supported by senior members of the judiciary and others who recognise that the capacity of the common law alone to protect human rights is limited. In particular, incorporation will mean that Government ministers must exercise their powers in accordance with the Convention.[60] The most sensitive question is the extent to which British judges should be empowered to ensure that primary legislation complies with the Convention.[61] More specifically, should they be given power to disapply or even strike down statutes which conflict with the Convention?

In the Community law context this problem has been addressed by means of the European Communities Act 1972. While that Act is not entrenched against repeal, it does require 'any enactment passed or to be passed' to 'be construed and have effect subject to' enforceable Community rights:[62] 'Under the terms of the 1972 Act it has always been clear that it was the duty of a United Kingdom court, when delivering final judgment, to override any rule of national law found to be in conflict with any directly enforceable rule of Community law.'[63]

As far as the incorporation of the European Convention is concerned, there are four main options.[64] In terms of ensuring that Convention rights have full force and effect in the United Kingdom, the best option would be to follow the pattern of the European Communities Act by providing that 'any enactment passed or to be passed' must be construed and applied subject to the Convention. This approach has a certain logic in that Convention

58 Ibid, p 72.
59 Announced in The Queen's Speech in May 1997.
60 Cf. *R* v *Secretary of State for the Home Department, ex parte Brind* [1991] 1 All ER 720.
61 See David Pannick QC, 'How to judge a human rights Bill', in *The Times*, 12 August 1997, p 33.
62 See especially ss 2(4) and 2(1) of the 1972 Act.
63 *Factortame Ltd* v *Secretary of State for Transport (No 2)* [1991] 1 All ER 70 at 108ab (*per* Lord Bridge).
64 Pannick, op cit. See further Ben Emmerson, 'This Year's Model – The Options for Incorporation' [1997] EHRLR 313.

rights already prevail over domestic legislation within the framework of Community law.[65]

The second option is to follow the Canadian approach. By virtue of s 52(1) of the Constitution Act 1982, any statute which is declared inconsistent with the Charter of Rights and Freedoms is, to the extent of the inconsistency, of no force or effect. In which case Parliament must either amend the impugned statute or re-enact it with an additional clause expressly stating that the relevant provision(s) shall operate notwithstanding the Charter. Such a clause has the effect of preventing the courts from disapplying the provision(s) in question.[66]

The third option is to follow s 6 of the New Zealand Bill of Rights Act 1990, which provides: 'Wherever an enactment can be given a meaning that is consistent with the rights and freedoms contained in this Bill of Rights, that meaning shall be preferred to any other meaning.' What that implies, however, is that if consistent interpretation is impossible, the statute must prevail – whether it was enacted before or after the Bill of Rights Act. In terms of the protection of human rights, that is the weakest option.

The fourth option is to adopt the approach advocated by Lord Lester of Herne Hill QC in his 1996 Human Rights Bill,[67] which preserves the doctrine of implied repeal.[68] Whereas *prior* legislation which could not be construed consistently with the Convention would be impliedly repealed, the British courts would endeavour to construe *subsequent* legislation[69] in accordance with the Convention. Only if they were unable to do so would the subsequent legislation prevail, leaving the aggrieved individual to seek redress in Strasbourg. The attraction of this approach is that it does not alter the constitutional relationship between Parliament and the judges.[70] It is true that where 'compliant construction' proved impossible, the British courts would be unable to give effect to Convention rights and freedoms. However, if a breach of the Convention were exposed by the judges and unaddressed by

---

[65] See Chapter 4.

[66] See s 33 of the Charter of Rights and Freedoms. See further John Wadham, 'Bringing Rights Half-way Home' [1997] EHRLR 141.

[67] See Lord Lester of Herne Hill QC, 'First Steps Towards a Constitutional Bill of Rights' [1997] EHRLR 124.

[68] See A W Bradley and K D Ewing, *Constitutional and Administrative Law* (Longman, 11th edn, 1993), pp 76–7.

[69] I.e. legislation passed after the Act incorporating the Convention into UK law.

[70] Pannick, op cit.

the government, the applicant would normally have 'an unanswerable case in Strasbourg'.[71]

Whichever model is chosen, comparisons with the European Communities Act are appropriate. For, as Lord Lester has observed, while the legislation incorporating the Convention into UK law will not be entrenched against amendment or repeal, British courts can be expected to regard it as a fundamental law having special constitutional status unless and until Parliament rules to the contrary.[72]

4.1 The Human Rights Bill

The Human Rights Bill, published in October 1997,[73] essentially follows the New Zealand approach. If it becomes law, the courts will have no power to strike down or set aside primary legislation (whether past or future) which conflicts with the Convention; however, they will be able to strike down incompatible secondary legislation unless they are prevented from doing so by the terms of the parent statute.[74] So far as possible, primary and secondary legislation will have to be interpreted and applied in conformity with Convention rights as defined in Strasbourg.[75] That rule of construction, which will apply to past as well as future legislation, goes far beyond the present rule which enables the courts to take the Convention into account in order to resolve ambiguity. They will be required to interpret legislation in accordance with Convention rights unless the legislation in question is so clearly incompatible with the Convention that consistent interpretation is impossible; that is, unless the legislation itself contains a clear limitation of Convention rights. Moreover, the courts will not be bound by previous interpretations of statute but will be able to

---

71 Ibid.

72 Lord Lester of Herne Hill QC, 'Twilight of our elective dictatorship', in *The Times*, 15 May 1997, p 20.

73 Cm 3782. See further 'Rights Brought Home: The Human Rights Bill' (Home Office, October 1997).

74 The 'European Communities Act' model was rejected on the grounds that it is a requirement of EU membership that Member States give priority to directly effective Community law in their own legal systems, whereas there is no such requirement under the Convention.

75 'Convention rights' means the rights and freedoms set out in Arts 2 to 12 and 14 of the Convention and Arts 1 to 3 of Protocol No 1, as read with Arts 16 to 18 of the Convention (subject to any designated derogation or reservation). Art 13 (the right to an effective remedy) is a notable omission.

build up a body of case law taking Convention rights into account.

If a higher court is satisfied that legislation is incompatible with Convention rights and consistent interpretation is impossible, it will be able to make a 'declaration of incompatibility'. While such a declaration will not affect the validity, continuing operation or enforcement of the legislation and will not be binding on the parties to the proceedings in which it is made, it will normally prompt a change in the law. Although the amendment of legislation will be a matter for Parliament, not the courts, the Human Rights Bill provides for fast-track remedial action to bring the law into line with the Convention: a Minister of the Crown will, by Order, be able to make such amendments as he or she considers appropriate; thus using secondary legislation to amend primary legislation.

It will be unlawful for a public authority[76] to act in a manner incompatible with Convention rights. Convention points will normally be taken in the context of proceedings instituted against individuals or already open to them, but in any event it will be possible to bring cases on Convention grounds alone. The Bill provides that individuals or organisations seeking judicial review of decisions by public authorities on Convention grounds will have to show that they are directly affected, as they must at present in order to take a case to Strasbourg.[77] A court or tribunal will be able to grant any remedy which is within its normal powers to grant and which it considers appropriate and just in the circumstances. For example, the decision of the public authority could be quashed or damages awarded.[78]

There are also important implications for the legislative process. The Minister in charge of a Bill will be required to make a written statement either that in his view its provisions are compatible with the Convention; or that although he is unable to make a statement of compatibility, the government nevertheless wishes to proceed with the Bill as it stands. The significance of this requirement is

---

[76] Defined broadly to include central government (including executive agencies), local government, the police, immigration officers, prisons, courts and tribunals, and, to the extent that they exercise public functions, companies responsible for areas of activity which were previously within the public sector, such as the privatised utilities.

[77] See Chapter 2. Cf. the proposal of the Bar's ECHR working group that, in order to ensure effective access to Convention rights, the more flexible 'sufficient interest' test used in judicial review proceedings should be applied.

[78] The amount of compensation being equivalent to that which the Strasbourg Court would have awarded.

twofold. First, a statement of compatibility will encourage the courts (if they need any encouragement) to construe the resulting statute in conformity with Convention rights. Secondly, any departure from the Convention is likely to be deliberate and reasoned: in the absence of a statement of compatibility, a Bill will undoubtedly be subject to careful Parliamentary scrutiny.[79]

4.2 The implications for the EU of the ECHR's incorporation into UK law

The legal and political significance for the EU of the incorporation of the European Convention into UK law should not be underestimated. Incorporation is likely to influence the political debate within the EU on the Communities' accession to the Convention. Furthermore, the fact that human rights will have a key place in the British constitution[80] reinforces the guarantees of the Treaty on European Union. It can only enhance the protection of human rights within the EU and strengthen the concept and culture of EU citizenship, thus helping to substantiate the Union's claim to be 'founded on the principles of liberty, democracy, respect for human rights and fundamental freedoms, and the rule of law, principles which are common to the Member States'.[81]

---

[79] Lord Irvine of Lairg, The Tom Sargant Memorial Lecture, 16 December 1997: *The Development of Human Rights in Britain under an Incorporated Convention on Human Rights* (The Lord Chancellor's Department, 1997).

[80] As Lord Irvine observes, incorporation represents a shift to a rights-based system of positive entitlements, away from the traditional view of liberty as the 'negative right' to do whatever is not prohibited.

[81] Art F(1), renumbered Art 6(1) TEU.

Further reading

A M Arnull, *Opinion 2/94 and its Implications for the Future Constitution of the Union*, in *The Human Rights Opinion of the ECJ and Its Constitutional Implications,* University of Cambridge, CELS Occasional Paper No 1, June 1996

I Cameron, 'Protocol 11 to the European Convention on Human Rights: the European Court of Human Rights as a Constitutional Court' (1995) 15 YEL 219

A Cassese, A Clapham and J Weiler (eds), *European Union – The Human Rights Challenge*, Nomos, Baden-Baden, 1991

A Clapham, 'A Human Rights Policy for the European Community' (1990) 10 YEL 309

J Coppel and A O'Neill, 'The European Court of Justice: Taking Rights Seriously?' (1995) 29 CMLRev 669

P van Dijk, *Judicial Protection of Human Rights in the European Union – Divergence, Co-ordination, Integration*, University of Exeter, Centre for European Legal Studies, Exeter Paper in European Law, No 1 (1996)

B Emmerson, 'This Year's Model – The Options for Incorporation' [1997] EHRLR 313

D J Harris, M O'Boyle, C Warbrick, *Law of the European Convention on Human Rights*, Butterworths, 1995

M Hunt, *Using Human Rights in English Courts*, Hart Publishing, Oxford, 1997

Lord Irvine of Lairg, 'The Development of Human Rights in Britain under an Incorporated Convention on Human Rights', Tom Sargant Memorial Lecture, The Lord Chancellor's Department, 1997

K Lester and D Oliver, *Constitutional Law and Human Rights*, Butterworths, 1997

Sir N Lyell QC, 'Whither Strasbourg? Why Britain Should Think Long and Hard before Incorporating the European Convention on Human Rights' [1997] EHRLR 133

P Twomey, 'The European Union: Three Pillars Without a Human Rights Foundation', in O'Keefe, Twomey (eds), *Legal Issues of the Maastricht Treaty*, Wiley Chancery, 1994

H G Schermers, 'The Eleventh Protocol to the European Convention on Human Rights' (1994) 19 ELRev 367

J Straw MP and P Boateng MP, 'Bringing Rights Home: Labour's Plans to Incorporate the European Convention on Human Rights into UK Law' [1997] EHRLR 71

J Wadham, 'Bringing Rights Half-Way Home' [1997] EHRLR 141

J H H Weiler and N J S Lockhart, ' "Taking Rights Seriously" Seriously: The European Court of Justice and its Fundamental Rights Jurisprudence' (1995) 32 CMLRev 51 (Part I), 579 (Part II)

Commission of the European Communities, *The protection of fundamental rights as Community law is created and developed*, Report of 4 February 1976, Bulletin of the European Communities, Supplement 5/76

Commission of the European Communities, *Accession of the Communities to the European Convention on Human Rights,* Memorandum of 4 April 1979, Bulletin of the European Communities, Supplement 2/79

Home Office, *Rights brought home: The Human Rights Bill*, October 1997

House of Lords Select Committee on the European Communities, *Human Rights*, Session 1979-80, 71st Report, HL 362

House of Lords Select Committee on the European Communities, *Human Rights Re-examined*, Session 1992–93, 3rd Report, HL Paper 10

Below are listed the main journals, law reports and internet addresses relating to European law and human rights.

Journals

The *European Law Review* covers the law relating to European integration and the Council of Europe. It is published six times a year. In addition, a human rights survey is published annually.

The *European Human Rights Law Review* seeks to promote better understanding of European human rights law and to provide a forum for serious debate on the European Convention on Human Rights. There are six issues per year.

See also the *Yearbook of European Law*, the *Common Market Law Review* and *Legal Issues of European Integration*.

Law reports

For the official reports of cases before the Court of Justice/Court of First Instance and the Court of Human Rights, see the *European Court Reports* (Office for Official Publications of the European Communities, Luxembourg) and the *Reports of Judgments and Decisions* (Council of Europe, Strasbourg), respectively.

See also the *Common Market Law Reports* (CMLR) and the *European Human Rights Reports* (EHRR), both published by Sweet & Maxwell. The CMLR cover decisions of national courts as well as those of the Court of Justice and Court of First Instance. The EHRR provide excellent coverage of cases before the Court and the Commission of Human Rights.

The Internet

European Court of Justice (including recent judgments):
   http://www.europa.eu.int/cj

European Court of Human Rights (including judgments, forthcoming cases and texts of European human rights law):
   http://www.dhcour.coe.fr

For information about the Council of Europe's structure, aims and activities: http://stars.coe.fr/gen/aintro.htm

Statewatch (monitoring the State and civil liberties in the EU):
   http://www.poptel.org.uk/statewatch

Bibliography

M K Addo, 'Justiciability Re-examined', in Beddard and Hill (eds), *Economic, Social and Cultural Rights: Progress and Achievement*, Macmillan, 1992, p 93

P Alston, 'A Third Generation of Solidarity Rights: Progressive Development or Obfuscation of International Human Rights Law?' (1982) 29 NILR 307

P Alston (ed.), *The United Nations and Human Rights, A Critical Appraisal*, Clarendon Press, Oxford, 1992

P Alston (ed.), *Human Rights Law*, Dartmouth, Aldershot, 1996

A M Arnull, 'Opinion 2/94 and its Implications for the Future Constitution of the Union', in *The Human Rights Opinion of the ECJ and Its Constitutional Implications*, University of Cambridge, CELS Occasional Paper No 1, June 1996

Abrahim Badawy El-Sheikh, 'The African Commission on Human and People's Rights: Prospects and Problems' (1989) 7 NQHR 272

R Beddard, *Human Rights in Europe*, Grotius, Cambridge, 3rd edn, 1993

L Betten, *International Labour Law: Selected Issues*, Kluwer, 1993 (2nd edn forthcoming)

L Betten and D MacDevitt (eds), *The Protection of Fundamental Social Rights in the European Union*, Kluwer Law International, The Hague, 1996

K A Betterman, F L Neuman and H C Nipperdey, *Die Grundrechte*, Berlin, 1966

B Boutros-Ghali, *The League of Arab States*, in *The International Dimensions of Human Rights*, Karel Vasak (ed.), Greenwood Press, 1982 (revised 1995/96)

A W Bradley and K D Ewing, *Constitutional and Administrative Law*, Longman, London, 11th edn, 1993

L Neville Brown, 'The first five years of the Court of First Instance and appeals to the Court of Justice: assessment and statistics' (1995) 32 CMLRev 743

L Neville Brown and Tom Kennedy, *The Court of Justice of the European Communities*, Sweet & Maxwell, London, 4th edn, 1994

I Brownlie (ed.), *Basic Documents on Human Rights*, Clarendon Press, Oxford, 3rd edn, 1992

I Brownlie (ed.), *Basic Documents in International Law*, Clarendon Press, Oxford, 4th edn, 1995

P Cane, *An Introduction to Administrative Law*, Clarendon Press, Oxford, 3rd edn, 1996

A Cassese, A Clapham and J Weiler (eds), *European Union – The Human Rights Challenge*, Nomos, Baden-Baden, 1991, 3 volumes

A Clapham, 'A Human Rights Policy for the European Community' (1990) 10 YEL 309

Commission of the European Communities, *The protection of fundamental rights as Community law is created and developed*, Report of 4 February 1976, Bulletin of the European Communities, Supplement 5/76

Commission of the European Communities, *Accession of the Communities to the European Convention on Human Rights*, Memorandum of 4 April 1979, Bulletin of the European Communities, Supplement 2/79

J Coppel and A O'Neill, 'The European Court of Justice: Taking Rights Seriously?' (1995) 29 CMLRev 669

M C R Craven, *The International Covenant on Economic, Social and Cultural Rights*, Clarendon Press, Oxford, 1995

A A Dashwood, 'Commentary', in *The Human Rights Opinion of the ECJ and Its Constitutional Implications*, University of Cambridge, CELS Occasional Paper No 1, June 1996

Lord Denning, *What Next In The Law?*, Butterworths, London, 1982

P van Dijk, *Judicial Protection of Human Rights in the European Union – Divergence, Co-ordination, Integration*, University of Exeter, Centre for European Legal Studies, Exeter Paper in European Law, No 1 (1996)

P van Dijk and G J H van Hoof, *Theory and Practice of the European Convention on Human Rights*, Deventer, 2nd edn, 1990

P Duffy, *The Human Rights Dimension To Competition Practice*, Lawyers' Europe (The Journal of the Solicitors' European Group), Summer 1994, p 6

C Duparc, *The European Community and Human Rights*, Commission of the European Communities, 1992

B Emmerson, 'This Year's Model – The Options for Incorporation' [1997] EHRLR 313

U Everling, 'Will Europe slip on bananas? The Bananas judgment of the Court of Justice and national courts' (1996) 33 CMLRev 401

S Farran, *The UK Before the European Court of Human Rights*, Blackstone Press, London, 1996

G Gaja, 'Opinion 2/94, Accession by the Communities to the European Convention for the Protection of Human Rights and Fundamental Freedoms' (with annotation) (1996) 33 CMLRev 973

Y Galmot, *L'apport des principes généraux du droit communautaire à la garantie des droits dans l'ordre juridique français*, (1997) 1-2 Cahiers de Droit Européen 67

G Gilbert and J Wright, 'The Means of Protecting Human Rights in the United Kingdom' (1997) 1 International Journal of Human Rights 23

N J Grief, 'The International Protection of Human Rights: Standard-setting and Enforcement by the United Nations and the Council of Europe' (1983) Bracton Law Journal 41

H Gros Espiell, *The Organisation of American States (OAS)*, in *The International Dimensions of Human Rights*, Karel Vasak (ed.), Greenwood Press, 1982, p 548

D J Harris, *The European Social Charter*, University Press of Virginia, 1984

D J Harris, *The Collective Complaints Protocol to the European Social Charter*, Council of Europe, *The Social Charter of the 21st Century*, Colloquy in Strasbourg, 14-16 May 1997 (Doc SCColl/rep1e)

D J Harris, M O'Boyle, C Warbrick, *Law of the European Convention on Human Rights*, Butterworths, 1995

A W Heringa, *Social Rights and the Rule of Law*, Council of Europe Colloquy on The Social Charter of the 21st Century, Strasbourg, May 1997, p 17 (Doc SCColl/rep9e)

House of Lords Select Committee on the European Communities, *Human Rights*, Session 1979–80, 71st Report, HL 362

House of Lords Select Committee on the European Communities, *Human Rights Re-examined*, Session 1992–93, 3rd Report, HL Paper 10

M Hunt, *Using Human Rights in English Courts*, Hart Publishing, Oxford, 1997

International Federation of Human Rights Leagues, *Observations on the revised European Social Charter*, Council of Europe Colloquy on The Social Charter in the 21st Century, Strasbourg, May 1997, p 9 (Doc SCColl/rep8e)

Lord Irvine of Lairg, 'The Development of Human Rights in Britain under an Incorporated Convention on Human Rights', Tom Sargant Memorial Lecture, The Lord Chancellor's Department, December 1997

F G Jacobs and R C A White, *The European Convention on Human Rights*, Clarendon Press, Oxford, 2nd edn, 1996

M W Janis, R S Kay and A W Bradley, *European Human Rights Law*, Clarendon Press, Oxford, 1995

B Kausikan, 'Asia's Different Standard', in Alston (ed.), *Human Rights Law*, Dartmouth, 1996, p 24

Lord Lester of Herne Hill QC, *General Report*, 8th International Colloquy on the ECHR (Budapest, 20–23 September 1995), Council of Europe

Lord Lester of Herne Hill QC, 'Twilight of our elective dictatorship', in *The Times*, 15 May 1997, p 20

Lord Lester of Herne Hill QC, 'First Steps Towards a Constitutional Bill of Rights' [1997] EHRLR 124

D McGoldrick, *The Human Rights Committee: Its Role in the Development of the International Covenant on Civil and Political Rights*, Clarendon Press, Oxford, 1994

D McGoldrick, *International Relations Law of the European Union*, Longman, 1997

C Medina, *The Battle of Human Rights: Gross, Systematic Violations and the Inter-American System*, Martinus Nijhoff, The Hague, 1988

T Meron (ed.), *Human Rights in International Law, Legal and Policy Issues*, Clarendon Press, Oxford, 1992

N A Neuwahl and A Rosas (eds), *The European Union and Human Rights*, Martinus Nijhoff, The Hague, 1995

M O'Flaherty, *Human Rights and the UN: Practice Before The Treaty Bodies*, Sweet & Maxwell, 1996

S O'Leary, 'Accession by the European Community to the European Convention on Human Rights – The Opinion of the ECJ' [1996] EHRLR 362

D Pannick QC, 'How to judge a human rights Bill', in *The Times*, 12 August 1997, p 33

B G Ramcharan (ed), *Human Rights, thirty years after the Universal Declaration*, Martinus Nijhoff, The Hague, 1979

Report of the Court of Justice on Certain Aspects of the Application of the Treaty on European Union, Proceedings of the Court of Justice and the Court of First Instance, No 15/95

Report of the High Level Panel on the free movement of persons chaired by Mrs Simone Veil, presented to the Commission on 18 March 1997

L Samuel, *Fundamental Social Rights: Case law of the European Social Charter*, Council of Europe, Strasbourg, 1997

H G Schermers, 'The Eleventh Protocol to the European Convention on Human Rights' (1994) 19 ELRev 367

L B Sohn, 'The Universal Declaration of Human Rights', Journal of the International Commission of Jurists, (1968) Special Issue 17

J Steiner and L Woods, *Textbook on EC Law*, Blackstone Press, 5th ed, 1996

J Straw MP and P Boateng MP, 'Bringing Rights Home: Labour's Plans to Incorporate the European Convention on Human Rights into UK Law' [1997] EHRLR 71

I Szabo, 'Historical Foundations of Human Rights and Subsequent Developments', in Vasak (ed.), *The International Dimensions of Human Rights*, Greenwood Press, 1982, vol 1, p 13

J Temple Lang, 'The Sphere in which Member States are Obliged to Comply with the General Principles of Law and Community Fundamental Rights Principles', LIEI 1991/2 23

P Twomey, 'The European Union: Three Pillars Without A Human Rights Foundation', in O'Keefe and Twomey (eds), *Legal Issues of the Maastricht Treaty*, Wiley Chancery, 1994

J A Usher, *General Principles of EC Law*, Longman, 1998

N Valticos and G von Potobsky, *International Labour Law*, Kluwer Law International, 1995

K Vasak (ed.), *The International Dimensions of Human Rights*, Greenwood Press, Westport, Connecticut, 1982 (2 vols)

R Vaughan, *Post-War Integration in Europe*, Edward Arnold, London, 1976

J Wadham, 'Bringing Rights Half-Way Home' [1997] EHRLR 141

J H H Weiler and N J S Lockhart, ' "Taking Rights Seriously" Seriously: The European Court of Justice and its Fundamental Rights Jurisprudence' (1995) 32 CMLRev 51 (Part I), 579 (Part II)

C E Welch Jr, *Protecting Human Rights in Africa*, University of Pennsylvania Press, Philadelphia, 1995

Index

153